D0006812

BROTHER FRANK

B Minucci F M382B
Minucci, Frank.
Brother Frank /

DEC — 1997

PROPERTY OF
HIGH POINT PUBLIC LIBRARY
HIGH POINT, NORTH CAROLINA

BROTHER FRANK

Frank Minucci
and William Hoffman

KENSINGTON BOOKS

http://www.kensingtonbooks.com

PROPERTY OF
HIGH POINT PUBLIC LIBRARY
HIGH POINT, NORTH CAROLINA

KENSINGTON BOOKS are published by

Kensington Publishing Corp.
850 Third Avenue
New York, NY 10022

Copyright © 1998 by Frank Minucci

All rights reserved. No part of this book may be reproduced in any form or by any means without the prior written consent of the Publisher, excepting brief quotes used in reviews.

Kensington and the K logo Reg. U.S. Pat. & TM Off.

Library of Congress Card Catalog Number: 97-072054
ISBN 1-57566-080-6

First Kensington Hardcover Printing: January, 1998
10 9 8 7 6 5 4 3 2 1

Printed in the United States of America

To my Beloved Wife Patricia,

If I could, I would put your face on the Statue of Liberty for all to see. For that is what your love, faith, and kindness have given me. The liberty and courage to come out from behind the walls that abuse, hate, and fear have kept me trapped behind for so long.

Thanks for loving me even when I didn't deserve it, and thanks for being my friend.

No one loves you more than me except God!

Always and then some,
Frankie

ACKNOWLEDGMENTS

Thanks to: My God.

A Special Thanks for your love and faith to: my sons, Angelo Minucci and Salvatore Marrazzo; Anthony and Anna Naimo; Pastors Fred and Judith Reinglas (they reached out when others turned away); Rev. Ralph and Lucy Romeo (they taught me to give without counting); Rev. Don Swantek (my brother from God); Pastor Carlos and Carmen Gracia; Pastor Charlie Rizzo; the late Dr. Norman Vincent Peale; Marlene and Joseph Canaan; and Rev. Stan Foster.

In Special Admiration: Peter E. DeBlasio P.C. His strength, wisdom, and integrity help shape my life.

A heartbeat to my Nomad brothers: Marty (Suds) Cassio, Don (Big Daddy) Emeroy, Ron (Ginzo) Dunaway, and all 360 of you!

A big thanks to: Bob Jacobs, NYPD. Without your skill and dedication, I wouldn't be here.

In memory of my infant daughter, the late Maria Antonette Minucci.

A heartfelt remembrance to the late Pastor Rev. Paul McCarthy, D.O. He put me in Bible school and taught me Faith.

The late Wayne Famular, "a brother and a friend."

The late Anthony Naimo, Jr., "Whose strength opened my eyes."

Thanks to my friends and agents in film: Bruce Kivo and Stanley Kaplin, and Bonnie Timmerman casting.

Last but not least, some friends and family whose kindness and loyalty deserve a grateful thanks: James (East Coast Jimmy) Antonietti, Larry Pesci (Gold Coast), Heather Hughes (niece), Frank Famular (The Famous One), Mike Lorito, James Howarth (NYPD), and Bobby (Moses) Schweikle.

To my godchild and niece, my darling Geena Francesca Bartolotta. I love you!

Thanks to Patrick and Francis Bartolotta, for making me a real Godfather.

To everyone else—Thank You and God Bless!

—Frank Minucci

As always, the book couldn't have been done without the love and help of Judy Hoffman.

I want to thank Lisa and William Hoffman III and Kasha Hoffman; Joe Hoffman; Julio and Terri Hoffman Escalante and James Patrick; John Hoffman; Alicia Lewis; Ethan Lewis; Micah Lewis; John and Anita Reeves; Ruby Lemon; Anna Lucy Wainwright; Margaret Rose Fagan Key; Joe and Linda Lewandoski; Dwight and Barbara Steward; Jim Gosdin; Birdie Segrest; Jim Lucas; Mike Stuhff; Jack and Jackie Grimm; Jerry and Jane Shields; Marty Reisman; Audra A. Ansley; Austin Adam; Margaret Wood; and Beth Stilley.

—W.H.

Chapter 1

The Minucci family tree, a shady one with roots deep in Sicily and La Cosa Nostra, branched to America when Grandfather brought my dad, Carmine, to New York City as a boy. Carmine's closest friend was young Carlo Gambino, who became head of the enormous crime family named for him, and the model for Marlon Brando's Don Corleone in *The Godfather.*

Carmine Minucci was a devoted family man but not in the typical sense. The family he worked day and night to support was exceedingly large and consisted of gangsters; his other family, a wife and three children at home, received only a tiny fraction of his attention. My early memories amount to seeing him dressed to the nines, stuffing expensive pockets with money, and leaving in his shiny new car "to conduct business."

The only father-son talk I recall occurred after saying I didn't like "Uncle" Carlo. Taking time to correct this unacceptable sign of disrespect, Dad told me, "Carlo, as a boy, was carefree and loved stickball. The life he chose has made him suspicious and treacherous. But don't forget, it has also made him very wise."

Carlo gave my family a swimming pool and our first TV. I think Dad loved him more than anyone. Even as an old man he talked about how smart Carlo was, and infinitely more enterprising than modern godfathers. "He got loyalty from his soldiers," Dad often said. "There weren't no rats back then."

My father had an arrest record as long as the Jersey Turnpike: bookmaking; hijacking; firearms violations; bootlegging; Mann Act offenses (using young girls for prostitution); extortion; and the big one that cost him nine years, assault on federal officers. They had caught him stealing racehorses, and the subsequent shootout left Dad's partner dead, a crony wounded, and charges even his powerful ally Carlo Gambino couldn't fix.

Dad was no small-potatoes thug. On November 14, 1957, he was one of sixty-three gangsters—including Chicago's Sam Giancana and four current and two future godfathers of New York City's five organized crime families—arrested at the National Mafia Commission meeting in Apalachin, New York.

In all likelihood I would have continued the Minucci male tradition and become a made guy, except for one thing: not being full-blooded Italian made me ineligible.

Dad stood just five-feet-one. He was powerfully built and extremely strong, handsome, with jet black hair, devious and fearless. When I say devious, I mean it. As an adult I seldom talked to him—maybe once every three months—and then only by phone. A call from him was usually a surprise, like the one in 1978.

"I've got bad news," he said. "Your mom died yesterday, and they're gonna bury her in potter's field. You oughta send me four thousand dollars so I can see she gets a decent funeral."

"You'll never guess who I saw today," I said.

"Who's that?"

"I'll give you a hint: a woman with red hair and green eyes."

Dad chuckled.

I hung up.

It was the rarest coincidence, seeing my mother that morning. I hadn't laid eyes on her for twenty-nine years. A friend had spotted her working in a Jersey department store, and for a hundred mixed-up reasons that I didn't understand, I went to see her. Ours wasn't one of those touching reunions you see on TV today, long-estranged mother and adult son rushing into each other's arms as a talk show host—perhaps Oprah—smiles proudly.

"I'm gonna tell you what I told your old man thirty-five years ago," Mom said icily. "There's nothing here for you. I'm looking out for Number One."

She spun on her heel and walked away, leaving me stunned, my mouth hanging open as a searing pain welled up inside me. I felt embarrassed and foolish; tears began to fill my eyes: it had just been confirmed as true what people had said about my mother not wanting me.

I screamed inside, "Mom, I love you!" but of course she didn't hear. And sad to say, I never laid eyes on her again.

My mom, Lucille O'Banion, was related to Dion O'Banion, described by author Stephen Fox in the book *Blood and Money* as "the most visible, powerful hoodlum in Chicago" in the early 1920s.

Whoever was responsible for the opposites attract theory must have known Lucille and Carmine. Born in Dublin, Ireland, she emigrated to the United States as a young girl and blossomed into a stunning beauty. When they met at Mardi Gras in New Orleans, the short swarthy gangster was captivated by the shamrock green eyes of the five-foot-ten feisty Irish lass. Convinced, probably correctly, that good looks and *amore* alone could not win this statuesque redhead's hand, he resorted to a more sinister tactic, based on the 1942 notion which dictated marriage as the socially acceptable solution to pregnancy. Carmine didn't succeed at Mardi Gras, but he kept trying. Finally she became pregnant (with me), wedding bells pealed, and the groom figured he had a trophy wife.

The honeymoon was short-lived. Mom and Dad fought all the time. No long, slow warm-ups with insults, pouts, or arguments; they *started* with screaming and cursing, quickly escalating to throwing fists, pots and pans, and lightweight furniture. Once Mom stabbed Dad in the chest with a pair of scissors after he found out about an affair she was having.

I was born on September 17, 1943, in Ashley, Mississippi, where my parents had moved temporarily so Dad could work on some Mob operations in Cuba. Before I reached my first birthday, we moved to Carteret, New Jersey, where my two sisters were born: Shirley, two years younger than me; and Karen, two years after that.

I do not have warm memories of childhood. My earliest memories are my parents fighting, Dad gone most of the time, and me and my sisters locked in a bedroom while Mom entertained other men. She never bothered to clean up her language, her three children, or the house; instead she spent hours primping in front of a mirror.

Occasionally, around age four, I accompanied Dad on his rounds: collecting vig on loans, picking up money from bookmakers, extorting protection payments from shopkeepers whose hands trembled with fear and rage. A few nights we drove with headlights off to a private airport and met a man who arrived in a plane. I sat in the car naively watching them load boxes into the trunk and Dad handing him a large paper sack—an exchange I eventually came to know as a contraband and counterfeit money deal.

Years later I told Dad I appreciated his taking me with him. I'd thirsted for *any* time I could spend with him. "Yeah," Dad replied, not understanding what I meant. "I took you along to take heat off myself. The cops never suspect a father and his little boy. Too bad your mother and I split up. Using your sisters as decoys might have kept me out of the slam."

Dad soon began disappearing for long periods of time and, finally, just dropped out of the picture. I learned he was in Roosevelt Hospital in Menlo Park, quarantined with TB.

That's when Mom really went bad, bringing a new man to the house almost every night. I'd bang on my bedroom door to get out, and she would come in, wearing only a loosely tied robe, slap my face, and scream, "I'm sick of you brats messing up my life!"

Once she pulled me out of the room and held my fingers to a fire on the stove burner until I passed out. After her male friend, who didn't raise a finger, left for the night, Mom stormed into the bedroom and beat my face with a shoe. "I hate you!" she said, locked the door, and headed for the neighborhood tavern.

I had several uncles I was always happy to see. I remember the day two of them stopped by for a visit and, after quickly tiring of Mom's yammering about too many kids making life miserable, decided to give her a dose of her own medicine. They locked *her* in the bedroom and took my sisters and me to a park.

I'd like to say Mom was crazy, but I just don't know. If so, she was evil-crazy. Instead of smothering us with kisses, she spit in our faces; instead of holding our hands, she stuffed our fingers in her mouth then bit down on them till they bled; instead of saying "I love you," she wished aloud that we were dead.

My sister Shirley, age three, was the first to be taken away from Mom. A horrified aunt took Shirley in and began raising her as her own. A few weeks later, another aunt took one-year-old Karen, which left me as the resident punching bag.

The daily routine never varied or improved. Confined to the house, I played quietly by myself through the morning while Mom slept off a hangover. She'd get out of bed in the afternoon and give me the silent treatment, her idea of punishment for something I'd done wrong. Every evening she locked me in my room and went out to drink and party. After the man she brought home left, she would unlock my door and look in on me. My mother, who was anything but motherly, didn't indulge in typical bedtime rituals of "Night-night, sweet dreams" wishes, a loving kiss on the cheek, and snugly tucking in her offspring. Instead, the last unsettling words I usually heard before going to sleep, sometimes cold and hungry, she snapped from the threshold: "You still alive? I was hoping you'd died."

One night unable to reach the bathroom in another part of the house, I messed my pants and hid under the bed hoping Mom wouldn't find out. She came home drunk, smelled the odor from my room, and screamed, "You stinking little monster, I'll kill you!" While I cowered out of sight, she got a mop and bucket and cleaned the floor. Then she pulled me by the hair from my hiding place, stood me in a corner, and began poking my stomach and ribs with the mop handle. I tried to curl into a ball but she kept finding places to jab. Next she dragged me to the bathtub, drew the water, and scrubbed me with a stiff-bristle brush. Suddenly she froze and I saw her contorted, evil expression change from hysterical to thoughtful. "This time I'm going to finish it," she said to herself, and put both hands atop my head, pushed down, and held my face under the water.

I guess for whatever reason—call it divine intervention, luck, or coincidence—that wasn't my night to die. The boyfriend she had been out with returned for something he'd forgotten, heard my mother's murderous screams, and pulled her off me.

I remember gasping for air and scrambling out of the tub across the floor. My mother screamed at her boyfriend, then punched and kicked him. "I hate him," she said, referring to me. "He's ruined my life. Let me kill the little . . ."

Confused, I lay on the cold floor wondering what I'd done to make my mother so angry. She must, I thought, have a good reason to despise me so much. My neck felt like it was on fire from the scratches of her long red fingernails, and my nose was bleeding as I cringed on the tile floor naked and wet.

Another time one of her severe beatings caused me to hemorrhage large clots of blood. When an aunt saw my condition and called a doctor to the house, Mom told him, "It would be better for everybody if he died."

Did this Hippocratic oath-taker try to rescue me from the clutches of an uncaring mother by calling social services or the police? No, quite the opposite. He started dating my mother, and when she finally ran away, it was with him.

Before that happened, however, the aunt who had taken one-year-old Karen returned her to Mom. This aunt, already overburdened by her own large brood, had tried to do what she called her Christian duty, but the addition of one more dependent proved too much for her. I knew she felt bad about bringing Karen back, but she didn't have another choice.

I remember Dad coming home from the Menlo Park hospital, and how thrilled and confident I was that he wouldn't let Mom beat me anymore. I stood at the door when he drove up, waiting for my savior to scoop me into his arms and hug me.

But my problems were not his concern. He'd only stopped by to pick up some of his things and confront Mom about her boyfriends, especially the doctor. He blew right by me and headed for Mom, who was talking on the phone. He ripped the receiver from her hand and hit her with it. "I should kill you!" he yelled, throwing her to the floor.

"Stop, Daddy!" I shouted. "Please, don't hurt Mommy!" I stood terrified, frozen at the door.

Mom pulled loose, blood trickling from her scalp, and fought like a tiger. They rolled on the floor, kneeing and punching, until Dad caught her in a right arm headlock and smashed her face with his left fist. She went limp but he continued the blows.

When he finally stopped, he let her sag to the floor, and hissed what had really been aggravating him: "You whore, you're a disgrace to my name."

I saw a pistol in his hand as he stood over my unconscious mom. "You're gonna die, tramp!"

"No, Daddy! No!"

He looked at me, ice in his eyes, no sign of recognition, then back at Mom. He knelt down and spit in her face. Then he smashed the butt of the gun twice against her bleeding skull and said something in Italian.

Police sirens brought Dad back to reality. He looked around, spit again in Mom's face, and while fleeing into the cellar, called over his shoulder, "I'll be back! I'll finish you *and* your boyfriend!"

A pair of cops burst into the kitchen. "Look at her!" one of them said, his voice full of horror. "Call an ambulance!"

The cop giving the orders headed for the cellar. I heard glass break, probably Dad crashing through a window; a gunshot, Dad firing at the officer; and two more shots, the officer shooting back.

Dad escaped, and the tough-as-nails niece of Dion O'Banion refused to help the police find him. Neither would I. One thing he taught me stuck my entire life: never snitch.

Mom suffered several skull fractures, a nose badly shattered, a broken jaw, and five broken teeth. She feared she would never regain her looks, but over the next several months, her future doctor husband, neurosurgeons, dentists, and a plastic surgeon rebuilt her almost to the beauty she once had been.

Dad crossed our portal only one more time, to retrieve the belongings he'd left behind in his earlier frenzied exit. Mom made sure not to be home when he came. "Dad, please," I begged, "take Karen and me with you."

"No," he said. "You belong to your mother."

Mom, the consummate good-time girl, didn't stop her partying to heal, but during this recuperative period a series of events occurred that took her out of our lives for good. Karen and I were left alone, locked in the house for almost three days, while she went to New York City with her doctor friend. I believe we might have died except for a freak episode. I was playing with the phone when an operator came on, questioned me, then called a neighbor on our party line.

The lady who came over to investigate gasped at the mess she found, and soon our house swarmed with people: police, child welfare, neighbors, a doctor—all of them making a tremendous fuss over Karen and me. I learned later that an APB was issued for Mom's arrest.

"We'll find you and your sister a nice home," a sweet-faced social worker said as we drove away.

Actually, our new home *was* nice, and the foster parents who took us in showered us with warmth and kindness.

For two weeks. Until the afternoon that Karen and I were playing in the frontyard.

All of a sudden, there was Mom. She picked up Karen, grabbed my hand, and tugged us toward the open door of a big black car. "Go!" she ordered the driver, once we were inside, and away we sped.

Why did Mom do it? Why did she snatch us? It took years for me to understand: she didn't care about our well-being, but we were *her* kids and neither the state nor anyone else had the right to decide what happened to us.

Our kidnapping, I found out later, became a minor sensation. Newspapers, radio, and TV trumpeted the big search launched for little Karen and Frank Minucci. If the Center for Missing Children had been active those days, my sister and I probably would have seen our faces on milk cartons.

We were driven to a large three-story white house surrounded by a big grassy lawn in need of mowing. The old paint-peeling structure in need of repair had once been a handsome home.

As we entered the house, Mom went to sit in a dimly lit living room and we were brought into the kitchen, where we were given a bowl of Crackerjacks to munch on.

Watching through the open kitchen door, I saw Mom hand a

woman named Edna a large wad of money, which the woman quickly put in her apron pocket. Several minutes later Mom came and took Karen and I to the backyard, where stood a rickety row of hutches filled with rabbits. Never having had a pet, Karen and I were entranced by their soft fur, cute ears, and constantly wiggling pink noses. The woman gave my sister and I a carrot to "feed the rabbits, honey," Mom said in a sweet voice. It was strange to hear Mom speak so polite and nice. It made me feel on edge; something was wrong.

Mom and the woman returned to the house, I cried out to her to stay with Karen and me but she just went in the house. I was drawn back by the rabbit, who seemed to like me and my carrot. In a short while, I remember becoming fearful. It was too quiet, and all of a sudden the reality set in—Mommy wasn't coming back.

Just then I heard a car motor start up in front of the house. My mind just seemed to explode with terror as I raced around the house, Karen toddling along behind. The women tried to grab me but I was too quick. Running up behind the car just as it pulled away, I cried out, "Mommy, Mommy, don't leave us."

"Go! Go!" my mother yelled at the driver, and the car sped away, throwing dust and cinders in my face. I fell face-forward onto the unpaved road, scraping my chin, knees, and arms in the cinders. I managed to look up just in time to see the car turning the far corner, and Mom pointing at me and laughing, "Good riddance, ya little bastard!" she yelled.

Everything got worse after Mom left. Edna took me inside and upstairs to a filthy attic. "You'll have to stay here for a while," she said. "Some bad people are looking for you. They're very mean. They'll hurt you if they find you."

Edna tied one end of a clothesline to my ankle and the other to the bottom of a bed frame covered with a thin dirty mattress in the center of the floor. "Now," she explained, "the bad people can't take you away and hurt you."

"Can I play with Karen?"

"Not now. The mean people want to steal her, too. I'll make sure she's safe."

I didn't believe Edna. I knew Karen would be crying and wondering where I was.

Actually, her circumstances, though horrible, were not as bad as mine. Only a year and a half old and unable to talk yet, Karen posed no threat to our captors, who told people they had adopted her. I, on the other hand, if allowed to roam free, might alert someone who would call the police.

For several months I saw Edna, and only Edna, twice a day. Mornings she brought me oatmeal and milk, which I ate after she took me to the bathroom. The meal at night was usually soup. When I asked about Karen, Edna either ignored the question or said to mind my own business, and to my complaints of being hungry, she replied, "Your mother isn't paying me enough to feed you any better."

I lost weight and became a miniature stick figure with a rib cage and shoulder blades protruding through a thin tight layer of unwashed skin that itched and cracked from head-to-toe rashes. It hurt to move.

Edna didn't like my crying. She would jab a cigarette at me, using it like a sword, demand that I shut up, and if I couldn't, she ground the cigarette out on my body.

I wrapped myself in fantasy. Lying on the bed, covered with sores, needing to go to the bathroom but forced to wait for Edna, I embraced a world of make-believe to keep from going crazy. I imagined breaking out of the attic, finding Karen, and taking her out of this dark nightmare into bright sunshine where we had lots of friends to play with and more food than we could eat.

Finally someone besides Edna came through the attic door: her husband Larry. I was glad to see him the first few times. He brought a Charlie McCarthy doll, and on another visit gave me a box of Crackerjacks. But the best gift of all was a potty chair he placed within my four-foot clothesline radius of the bed. Still, nothing could really calm my terror.

The attic, no doubt about it, was a scary and lonely place filled with strange noises that came from its dark corners. I spent many hours beneath my blanket afraid of the monsters that lurked in the shadows. The only person I now saw was Larry. He spoke softly and hugged me and told me he was my secret friend. He would lay me down in front of him and slide up behind me and pull me into his arms. He rubbed me all over, and his comforting made me feel warm and secure. He told me how bad Edna was, that he didn't like her either, that she didn't want him to be my friend so we had to keep everything a secret or she wouldn't let him visit anymore. He hugged me again and I promised I wouldn't tell.

The sexual abuse started on Larry's fourth visit with a game he called "Shooting Our Guns." We would take our pants off and pee at the potty to see who could shoot straight. Larry would kneel behind me, reach around and take hold of my "gun," and say he was helping me aim. He insisted that I also aim his "gun," which he called "the big one."

Often he rubbed my behind with his gun, saying he was shining it, and telling me these were the things friends did when they wanted to stay together forever.

The day soon came when Larry got rough. He was talking strange, smelling funny (he'd gotten drunk), and telling me today would be very special. He laid me on my stomach and rubbed something greasy on my bottom. When he lowered himself on top of me, I screamed out in pain.

Larry pushed me down and covered my mouth with his hand. He kissed my cheek, his breath stinking and his beard hurting my face. "Shut up!" he said, feeling the sobs behind the hand he'd clamped over my mouth. "Shut up, or I'll never be your friend again."

After he had finished sodomizing me, he told me it was called . . . love!

I was 5½ years old.

I did get taken from my attic prison on a few special occasions— special for Edna and Larry, that is. Usually I could identify the event by songs, "Silent Night" or "Happy Birthday." On these days, before the guests arrived, Edna and Larry transferred me to a more soundproof cell where I couldn't send an SOS by stomping my feet or banging the iron bed frame on the wood floor.

In the dank concrete cellar, they used an electrical extension cord to bind me securely, stuffed a washrag in my mouth, and locked me in a closet filled with mops and brooms at the bottom of the stairs. One afternoon I messed myself, as I once had when Mom was away, and Edna called me "a pig." She added, "This is what I get for taking care of you," and whipped me hard with the electrical cord.

I had withered to a repulsive bag of bones with open sores oozing body fluid, but Larry never stopped coming for sex. In order to survive the pain and humiliation, my mind dissociated. I mentally left my body and imagined myself somewhere else.

There was no sense of time. Only later did I learn that my captivity lasted eighteen months.

Liberation day began with Edna saying, "We're having friends over, but if you promise to behave yourself, you can stay up here."

She just didn't want to be bothered untying and tying me, having to drag me down to the cellar. "Look what I brought you," she said, producing a coloring book and crayons from behind her back. "You can play with these if you promise to be good." I was overjoyed. This was one of three toys I ever received from Edna. The other two were a tiny tin car and a little yellow tin duck.

I promised. The cluttered, dusty attic was paradise compared to that cellar closet.

Soon I heard sounds of merriment out in the yard, adults greeting one another, and giggling children at play—voices that seemed to beckon me to join them in the fun.

I tried to untie the knots in the clothesline but couldn't. Easing off the bed, I attempted to pull it with my foot over to the window, but the heavy bed seemed anchored to the floor and wouldn't budge. Stupidly I strained and yanked, the cord cutting deeper into my ankle, and I had to bite my lip to keep from crying out in pain. I tugged again, with all my might, and the bed moved a fraction of an inch. I willed my body not to feel pain and heaved again.

This won't work, I said to myself. *You'll rip your foot off before you reach the window.* Then the idea hit me—so simple, yet I'd overlooked it—and, sitting on the floor, I bent at the waist and pulled the rope with my hands. Coordinating weakened muscles, I scooted my rear backward and pulled the bed bit-by-bit toward the window. When I thought it was close enough, I started to stand up, reached a squat position, and fell on my face. Dust filled my nostrils and mouth.

I finally reached the window, but was at first too terrified to look out. What if Larry or Edna saw me? Edna would beat me, burn me, then lock me in the closet in the cellar.

Crouching beneath the window, listening to sounds of gaiety alien to my life, I found myself almost paralyzed by fright. Tears streamed down my face as I lifted myself up to take a peek.

My eyes searched frantically for Edna, and found her stretched out in a lawn chair. Larry sat nearby drinking beer with a couple of male friends. My gaze flashed from person to person, heart racing with excitement at seeing the fun they were having, all the children running and playing. I saw a boy my age bite into a hot dog, a sight that almost drove me mad, and I stared enviously at the red-and-white-checked tablecloth on a picnic table displaying heaping bowls of chips, potato salad, cole slaw, baked beans, and fresh fruit. Aching to run and jump, join the backyard volleyball game, I forgot the pain in my corded ankle and even the ever-present emptiness in my heart.

Focusing on a mother hugging her baby, I began to weep.

A teenage girl looked up and saw me. I pulled back from the window, dropped onto my stomach, and rolled under the bed, terrified. I knew I'd done something "bad." The girl had to be a member of the "evil ones" Edna had warned about.

In a few minutes I heard someone coming up the stairs. *Oh, please, let it be Edna.* I thought she'd burn me with a cigarette, but that beat falling into the hands of the evil people. Warm urine soaked my pants as the footfalls drew closer.

The sight of an unfamiliar pair of shoes, walking slowly around the room and stopping beside the bed, told me the worst had happened. Then I gasped and shuddered when the upside-down eyes of the girl from the yard peered into mine. I thought my heart would explode.

"Good Lord!" she said. "What have they done to you?"

I hid my face in my hands.

"Come out of there," she coaxed gently.

"Go away," I cried.

She was pretty, her long hair collecting dust off the floor as she reached her hand out to me. My own hand went out, reflexively, and she pulled me out and on to my feet. Quickly scanning the sores and burn marks, she said, "You poor little thing," and enfolded me in her arms. I could feel her sobbing.

"What's your name?"

"Fra . . . Frankie."

"Frankie," she said, holding me at arm's length and whispering cautiously, "listen very carefully. Don't tell Edna or Larry that I was here. I'll come back, as soon as I can, with help."

But no help came that afternoon or evening. After dark, when the friends and neighbors had left, I fell asleep and dreamed of monsters.

Early the next morning Edna rushed into my room, wearing an expression of dread instead of the usual loathing. "The bad people are here," she said, frantically untying the clothesline. "Don't say a word or they'll hear you and take you away."

She carried me under her arm like a football down the steps to the cellar, then hurriedly bound, gagged, and deposited me in the mop closet and shut the door. "Don't make a sound," she said, "or the bad people will cut you up and eat you."

After she left, I heard commotion overhead, doors opening and closing, heavy footsteps, gruff voices issuing terse orders. Next came a stampede of people tromping down the stairs.

My body shook. Hot tears made stinging tracks down my rash-reddened cheeks, and I squeezed my eyes shut in the childish hope that if I couldn't see them, they couldn't see me. I wanted to be invisible to the "bad people."

Confusion and noise filled the tomblike cellar as my tortured mind prayed desperately *not* to be rescued. Jars and bottles clattered, hinges creaked until, finally, in a split second of silence, I felt exposed.

"See, I told you he was here. I told you so." I recognized the voice of the teenage girl and opened my eyes.

A big uniformed policeman towered over my cringing body. "What in the world . . ." he muttered. "Animals!"

The girl removed the gag from my mouth—"You're gonna be okay, Frankie," she said—and the officer scooped me up and carried me upstairs, still loosely bound by the extension cord, and set me down on a couch. People hovered everywhere, and a man in a suit—a doctor, I think—knelt in front of me and gently probed my body.

A scuffle broke out. Only many years later did I learn that the cop had freaked out, drawn his gun, and threatened to blow Edna away. Three other officers had wrestled him to the floor.

"You were the most pitiful sight I've ever seen," this savior cop told me when as an adult I looked him up and became a friend of his.

My own memories were mainly of people shaking their heads and staring at me. I saw Larry and Edna, in handcuffs, being pushed out the front door.

An ambulance drove Karen and me to the hospital. She remained for seventy-two hours for "observation."

I was listed in critical condition for the first four days, hooked up to all sorts of machines and tubes while the doctors and nurses treated the most urgent ailments—pneumonia, dehydration, and malnutrition. During the three-week confinement they fixed my broken nose and helped heal the bedsores, skin rashes, and forty-plus burn marks on my arms, legs, and torso. Best of all, I received plenty of loving care. A cheerful dietician vowed to "put meat" on my bones, and my distended stomach returned to normal.

I was far into adulthood before I faced what had occurred and summoned the courage to search back and discover what happened to my abusers: Larry and Edna were sentenced to three years in prison; Mom did three and a half.

This is the first time I have revealed what went on in that attic. I've been tortured by the events for almost five decades now, and hope that telling about them will bring some closure.

The fact is, I feared that telling the story would be more frightening than living it. I kept the suffering bottled up inside the fortress I have hid in all my life, always thinking that what happened branded me as weak.

But my crying behind the fortress wall was finally heard: by my beloved wife Patty, and by my Lord and God.

Chapter 2

Click-click, click-click, click-click echoed the staccato double-time rhythm of Karen's tiny dress shoes on the marble floor. She and I, hand-in-hand, were following Mrs. Shoemaker's bulging briefcase to the office of the Bureau of Child Welfare in New Brunswick, New Jersey. Halting the march in front of a wooden bench against the wall, Mrs. Shoemaker, the social worker assigned the seemingly impossible task of finding the Minucci wards of the state a permanent residence, shot us a you-know-the-drill visual command and walked over to one of many desks in the large room.

I helped my sister climb into place and sat down beside her on the bench we had warmed too many times. Neither of us understood how the child welfare system worked, but we both knew that coming here with Mrs. Shoemaker meant relocation, placement in another strange house with people we had never seen before.

After our release from the hospital, Karen and I had been moved in and out of several different foster homes. Although our vagabond existence must have been hard on Karen, she didn't show it, and obediently went along with whatever program the government offered. I wasn't nearly as passive. At age eight I already had been earmarked a "problem child."

Today's trek to the agency was the worst yet, because Mrs. Shoemaker had removed us from people we loved: our great-aunt and great-uncle, who had taken us in temporarily while the search proceeded for foster parents who would keep us on a permanent basis.

Aunt Angelina and Uncle Ralph lived in Carteret, New Jersey, near the old train yards, property now occupied by the Hess Oil Company. Even though this older neighborhood of retirees offered no playmates, Karen and I were happy and content. We loved playing games with each other and the eight stone lions in the yard. Uncle Ralph, a kindly man, encouraged our outdoor activities: "The sunshine is healthy, and it's safe here."

Sicilian-born Aunt Angelina spoke no English but the words accompanying her nurturing caresses were a universal language of love and needed no translation from Uncle Ralph. A very religious woman in her late seventies, she displayed statues of Christ and Mary and pictures of the saints throughout the house. When we didn't see her cooking or cleaning, we could always find her praying at the small altar in the bedroom where candles burned at all times.

When Mrs. Shoemaker had knocked on the door this morning, Aunt Angelina hugged us and Uncle Ralph translated her gentle parting words: "Be happy, my children, and God keep you both."

After we left the Bureau of Child Welfare, Mrs. Shoemaker drove for a long time, and said more than once, "I think you'll love your new home in the country."

I wondered. Sure, as the "problem child" I shouldered much of the blame for our previous failures, but it was equally true that most of those homes had been hastily chosen and hardly populated by people with a special love for children. Some, who wanted newborns but were tired of the long wait, settled for us, and weren't able to cope with the ugly emotional baggage I brought along; most, however, were in the "racket" to receive a monthly stipend from the state, and weren't qualified caregivers by anyone's definition.

Our new country home was a mini-farm complete with chickens, ducks, geese, pigs, and rabbits (bloodcurdling reminders of our first day at Edna's place). Mr. and Mrs. Klein—old-fashioned, strict, honest, frugal Germans who had fled the ruins of war and established a new life in Colonia, New Jersey—seemed genuinely happy to see us.

Mr. Klein worked as an inspector at Worthington Pump; Mrs. Klein stayed at home, tending the garden and animals, and ran the show. The bald husband and his stocky wife were short, rosy cheeked, wholesome types with a scrubbed-clean orderliness about themselves and their surroundings.

My first year on the farm was governed by the strict Klein regimen: chores at sunrise, school, more chores, homework, and an inflexible 8 P.M. bedtime. My foster parents expected me to study, work the garden, tend the animals, and train for a technical vocation. No slack existed in Pop Klein's make-hay-while-the-sun-shines schedule to goof off, and playtime had to be earned. My reward for hard work and good behavior was one free afternoon on alternate weekends to play sports. But I never had a glove or bat or ball because my guardians considered it wasteful to spend money on toys.

I was a restless, rebellious, wise-mouth nine-year-old with a chip on my shoulder, always looking for and finding plenty of fights, usually precipitated by other children calling us the "Kraut kids," or the "orphans," or making fun of our outdated, corny state-issued clothes. When I came home wearing a shiner or bloody nose, Pop Klein slapped me on the back of the head, or beat me with whatever was in reach: a shovel, rake, broom, belt, or his favorite, a three-foot length of rubber hose.

Pop Klein meant well; he didn't know any other method of discipline.

Karen adapted much better than I did. In their way, the Kleins loved both of us, but Karen toed the line, and I didn't. Pop wasn't going to change, and as we would both finally have to admit, neither was I. So, the more punishment he dished out, the more rebellious I grew.

By the time I entered adolescence—in 1956—rock and roll was here to stay, and so was the new culture surrounding it: "cool" clothes, unconventional hairdos, hot rod cars, and hip talk. A year earlier Bill Haley and His Comets had pressed the first album of the new music era, "Rock Around the Clock," and teens were still jumping to the group's "Shake, Rattle and Roll." Jerry Lee Lewis had "Great Balls of Fire" and a "Whole Lotta Shakin'" going on. In September an estimated 54 million people—shrieking girls and blushing parents—watched the hip-swiveling gyrations of Elvis Presley on *The Ed Sullivan Show*.

Boys couldn't wait to grow Elvis sideburns, and our macho haircuts and fashion—jeans with smokes rolled in a white T-shirt sleeve—were copied from actors such as James Dean, Marlon Brando, and Tony Curtis. Determined to be a part of the scene, I came home one day with a slicked-back ducktail, and Pop blew his cork. He beat me all around the yard with that rubber hose; but I was growing tall and strong now, and we both suspected this couldn't go on much longer. "Wash that grease out of your hair and get your butt to the kennel!" he ordered.

Twice a day I had to feed the nine hunting dogs he bred and raised, clean their pens, and brush their coats. Being with them so often, naturally I broke another Klein commandment: "Don't get attached to the animals; they're here as an investment, not pets." The hounds came to love and trust me because, I think, they were, like me, starved for attention. I talked and they listened.

We had one oddball dog, a very vicious deaf dalmatian stray that someone had mistreated. Pop, the classic utilitarian, decided he'd make a good watchdog and told me to stay away from him. Instead, the dalmatian became my secret pal. I named him Junior, and before Pop got off work, I sneaked Junior out for romps through the woods, at the risk of getting beaten.

Searching for friends, I joined gangs such as the Hobo Lords, then El Diablos, and finally pledged my undying allegiance to the Sportsmen. Before long I was stealing cars, burglarizing houses, and skipping school.

At age fifteen I stood five-feet-eleven, weighed 165 pounds, and had earned a reputation as a ferocious fighter. My best friends were Bernie, also fifteen, a rich kid who hated his accordion lessons, and Hank, seventeen, the first of our crowd to own a car: a '57 Plymouth Fury he rebuilt in his father's garage.

Soon I began living at Hank's house with the approval of his mom, who disliked Pop Klein's strict disciplinary methods. About a week later, Pop came over yelling at her: "Mind your own business! Send the boy home where he belongs!" I ran out the back door and far into the woods.

Pop, marching behind his dalmatian on a choke chain, tracked me down. When Pop spotted me, he unsnapped the leash and signaled the dog to attack. Junior charged in my direction, growling lowly, his teeth bared. I knelt down, stretching my arms out to him, and his tail began wagging. He jumped on me and licked my face. Pop, outraged, came charging, brandishing a large stick over his head, swearing to kill me.

Junior attacked *him*. Eventually, I went home and got a beating, but I imagine Junior took as much satisfaction as I did from resisting Pop.

I tried another stint with the Kleins. Finding it unbearable, I started sleeping at the homes of friends and grubbing for handouts. This time Pop sent child welfare after me, and the counselor who caught me laid it on the line: "You either go to school, or end up as an incorrigible in juvenile hall."

It took less than a month for that to happen. Judge Appleton— reasoning that a foster brother my own age might improve my disposition—found me a new home. It didn't work there, either. The foster brother constantly insulted me and kept squealing to his parents whenever I sneaked out at night. I ended up punching him and kicking him down a flight of stairs.

Still convinced of her peer theory, the judge ordered another foster home. More trouble: I seriously beat the resident teenager and wrecked his expensive model trains. Judge Appleton, bless her heart, did her best to find me a place to live, but nothing seemed to work out. I was miserable and so were the people charged with caring for me. The truth is, I hated almost everyone.

Without excusing my own actions, I think it's safe to say the foster care system was (and sad to say, still is) a scandalous mess. Time and again people took me in, and the results were disastrous. Most of the foster parents I lived with (the Kleins were the exception) became involved with children like me for selfish reasons: financial, emotional, sexual. I lived with people who beat me, starved me, abused me sexually—and I don't think the system really cared. I was a bothersome, embarrassing piece of unwanted baggage the state wished it could simply make disappear.

After *thirteen* foster homes and several stays in Juvenile Delinquent Hall, I ended up in Jamesburg Reformatory. I was sixteen years old.

In handcuffs, pressure belt, and leg shackles, I was transported in a state car under a huge archway to a cluster of drab structures planted in the middle of fields stretching to a bleak horizon banked with dark snow clouds. From the backseat I saw rows of brick buildings and columns of marching boys, heads shaven, hard faces, dressed in khaki clothes and Ike jackets.

I was stripped, showered, sprayed with a de-licing disinfectant; handed a brown paper sack, folded and stapled at the top, containing toothpowder, toothbrush, bar soap, comb, two sheets of writing paper, one envelope, plus a set of rules and regulations; and assigned a shower room locker and a cot in a dorm, where I fell asleep.

The next day, awakened at 6 A.M., I soon found myself on my knees, snow blowing in my face, digging potatoes out of frosty soil. For seven hours—with a single break for a bologna sandwich and a cup of hot tea—we crawled through a bitterly cold field filling burlap bags with spuds.

The guards, called "cottage fathers," were mostly failed farmers or wannabe cops who tried to imitate Edward G. Robinson: "You're gonna do it my way, see." These largely illiterate bullies enjoyed spraying prisoners with cold water and then locking them outside in the wintry weather.

Jamesburg "Reformatory" resembled a hard-time penitentiary: in other words, it was a crime school warehousing troubled, rebellious youngsters and graduating hardened criminals. Older boys raped younger ones and the guards did nothing. If a young victim complained, *he* got punished. "You little liar," the guard would say, "are you telling me this happened on *my* shift? Are you trying to get me in trouble?"

Two boys were beaten to death while I was there and the killings got hushed up. Inmates were strapped to an official whipping post and flogged for crimes like sassing a guard, smoking, or tardiness.

Seventy boys, ages eight to eighteen, lived in each of the dozen "cottages" at Jamesburg. The building I lived in, which was pretty much the norm, housed sixty-four blacks, four whites, and two Puerto Ricans.

Jamesburg didn't have fences. A few German shepherds patrolled the grounds, but the real security came from nearby farmers, who received rewards for nabbing escapees. A lot of boys, driven by desperation, tried to escape, but only a few succeeded.

I escaped as soon as I could. On the way to the auditorium for the weekly movie, I jumped out of line and hid behind a snowdrift. Two hours passed before they missed me at bedcheck.

My escaping was no lark. I knew if they caught me, I might be killed. I lay in the snow until the spotlights were switched off, then ran for the fields behind the barns. Heart racing, I felt a sense of joyful excitement, racing across the snow. I slapped myself five when I reached the woods, and let out a yelp of joy.

Walking and hitchhiking my way to Colonia, half frozen when I arrived, I stayed with various friends until my welcome ran out with their parents, who thought I'd been legally released from Jamesburg. Finally, with no place else to go, I headed for Pop Klein's. He and Mom welcomed me, Karen hugged me warmly, and we had a nice family dinner.

The police picked me up the next morning. Pop had turned me in. Angry, hurt, and betrayed, I nursed a grudge against him for a long time. Many years later I told him how much I'd been hurt, and he apologized. "You were a fugitive," he explained in his still-broken English. "I was afraid if they found you at home, they would take Karen away from us."

Back at Jamesburg, one of the few things inmates looked forward to was the quarterly release hearing. I always got turned down. Even if they had wanted to let me out, they couldn't. I had nowhere to go, nobody wanted me. So they would postpone my release by tacking on another ninety days, and three months later we went through the motions again.

The only thing I did enjoy about this isolated place was the theater. Surprisingly, Jamesburg did have one source of culture: part-time volunteer acting coach George Yarrick. This Princeton drama professor for some reason took an interest in me, and I've never forgotten him. The soft-spoken, patient, compassionate Mr. Yarrick was one of the few people who truly cared about the kids at Jamesburg. He often stood up for us against the administration.

An alternative to working the fields was to study acting. Reasoning that figuratively breaking a leg would be far less painful than literally breaking my back at manual labor, I auditioned for and won several roles: Birdie's manager in *Bye, Bye, Birdie;* the lead in *It's Never Too Late;* and Hans Gruber in *Silent Night.* Twelve hundred people filled the auditorium for each of these productions and I loved the attention and applause. At the end of *Silent Night,* bathed in a pale blue spotlight, I recited the lyrics of the familiar carol while the off-stage reformatory glee club hummed the melody. The tough audience gave me a standing ovation. When the curtain came down, George Yarrick said, "You may be a natural for the acting business. You ought to consider it as a career when you get out."

Thirty years passed before I heeded his advice.

The average stay at Jamesburg was eight months; six months for good behavior. Altogether I spent twenty-two months there. Eventually, after seven turndowns, I got released to the probation department and moved into the Packard House hotel in Perth Amboy. I paid $15 a week for the tiny room, and worked at a state-arranged job at a shoe factory, soling ballerina slippers for $1.15 an hour.

It didn't take a math genius to figure out I'd never get anywhere at this rate, so at night I robbed houses, stole cars, and pulled several stickups. If nothing else, Jamesburg had taught me how to survive on the street. Some of the veteran thieves advised, "Save your house burglaries for Fridays—payday. And don't fool around with no old cars—new ones are just as easy to grab and turn a lot bigger profit."

Holdups were simpler in those days because of the large number of Mom and Pop businesses that had no alarm systems or safes, and police communications weren't very sophisticated.

I stayed on the streets for three months and committed perhaps fifty felonies before getting busted on a minor charge. At 3 A.M. I was walking a friend home, crossing railroad tracks behind a factory, when the police arrested us. The suspicion of attempted robbery charge didn't stick, but one for parole violation (being out at 3 A.M.) sent me back to Jamesburg for another three-month hitch. My parole officer said I had a "behavioral problem." True enough.

It wasn't long before I was in trouble again, but this time I found a way out. I had just turned eighteen, and the judge gave me a choice between joining the army—"That'll straighten you out, if anything can"—and going to Annandale reformatory.

I chose the army. I was the best of soldiers, and the worst. Best, because I was gung ho, loved the weapons and war games, would have been the guy to charge up hills at machine gun nests. Worst, since I had no discipline, hated taking orders, and often was drunk, AWOL, or stealing something. During boot camp I shot some snob rich kid in the rear during a simulated attack where smoke bombs were used. I got off by claiming I'd been blinded.

When I wasn't stealing weapons and selling them to a local Army-Navy store, I took vehicles from the motor pool and raced them on the airstrip behind the base.

Everybody in my unit except me got shipped to Europe. I was assigned to Army Chemical Center in Belair, Maryland, where the army gave me a special clearance as a "technical escort" to guard various secret projects they were working on.

Less exotic was the maintenance detail I often found myself assigned to, raking leaves and performing yardbird duties. Once, sitting beneath a tree, I heard a twig snap behind me, then, "On your feet, soldier!"

A ninety-day-wonder lieutenant had sneaked up on me.

I gave a good imitation of a hundred-year-old man rising to his feet and stood slumped in front of him.

"Stand at attention when an officer addresses you!" he tried to growl, but his prep school voice gave him away. "What are your orders, soldier?"

"Rake up leaves in front of HQ, sir."

"Anyone tell you to take a nap? To sit down? To smoke a cigarette?"

"No, sir." I almost choked on the "sir."

"Soldier," he said, "you need to be taught a lesson."

He grabbed the rake from my hands and slammed the handle hard into my chest.

"Return to . . ." he said, and got no further. I popped him on his pointed preppy nose.

"You've made a serious mistake," he said, but not before he'd picked himself up and put thirty feet between us.

I was court-martialed, but let off with merely a fine. It turned out the lieutenant shouldn't have hit me with the rake.

About a month after my court-martial, I called home to find that some kid had tried to rape my sister Karen. That night, I left the base without permission and the next day I was sitting in Woodbridge, New Jersey, jail for attempted murder. I tried to slice this guy's throat but missed and cut his cheek open instead. He got over two hundred stitches. But as soon as my sister filed rape charges against him, he dropped his claims against me and I was sent back to the army base. AWOL.

They sent me to a psychiatrist, who judged me "unable to adapt to military life," but a captain who liked my fearless attitude intervened and I was spared a dishonorable discharge. "He could be a good soldier, but we stuck him in an administrative position," the captain judged.

My next stop was Annandale.

This time out I supplemented my minimum wage job at an auto parts store by hooking up with Tony Santa, a friend from the Pop Klein days. We became a two-man crime wave. My goals in life: accumulate a lot of stuff; become the coolest of the cool. I bought a 1953 Mercury with a Plexiglas roof, Continental kit, and cruiser skirts. I tooled around in the sharp, fast car, and pretty soon peers began to recognize, if not admire, me as an important force.

I estimate Tony and I committed more than a hundred felonies, fencing some of the loot, impressing girlfriends with lavish presents, even passing out television sets to their parents, who didn't question how we could afford such gifts. Tony and I stole anything valuable.

Once we robbed all three houses on a suburban block in the same night; another time we had a running shootout with a home-owner who was supposed to be out of town; we even hit the mansion of a made mob guy—he didn't call the police, but we suspected that if he learned our identities we'd wished he had. A number of our burglaries netted many thousands of dollars in jewelry.

We were tipped off to good scores by an insurance agent in Scotch Plains who had written homeowner policies covering valu-ables. Paying 25 percent for his services was a "business expense" we were willing to absorb. "Like the pros say," I told Tony, "you gotta spend money to make money."

The police didn't know who was committing these robberies, but at the top of their short list of possibles were Tony Santa and Frank Minucci. They made no bones about suspecting us: "We're gonna catch your butts," a detective told me, "and then all you'll be cleaning out is a toilet bowl at Bordentown." I learned this detective had even given me a nickname, one I sort of liked: Fox.

Tony decided to cool it for a while and visit his father in Virginia. We agreed he should take the unfenced jewelry with him, get it out of New Jersey. He said, "I'll be back in a month."

Four weeks later I sat in Troopers, a pool hall and pizza joint, waiting for him. Two detectives showed up instead.

"Minucci," one of them said, "we've got a warrant for your arrest."

I brought the chair I was sitting on around and hit one of the cops in the chest, knocking him into the other. Someone told me later that I looked like Superboy leaping over a pool table and racing out the front door. By the time the cops recovered, I was gone.

The police knew my car, so I contacted a girlfriend, Mary, and persuaded her to loan me her wheels. I went into hiding, and managed to learn quickly what had happened. Tony Santa had gotten caught pulling a stickup in Virginia, and when the cops took a search warrant to his father's home, they found our jewelry stash. A few phone calls later and Tony was on his way back to Jersey in cuffs and shackles. Slippery as an eel, he briefly escaped out a window of the Rahway courthouse when the officer guarding him briefly turned his back, but Tony didn't get far. Now, I learned, he was being held in deep lockup.

I should have split for parts unknown, but I was young and dumb so I hung around. I dumped my car, bought a red and white Ford Vicky, and tried to avoid Union County.

A month later at the Four Seasons diner outside Rahway, the cops surprised me with guns drawn and shouts of "Freeze, punk!" As they handcuffed me, an officer named Charlie Gifford stood in my face, smiling smugly. "Hey, Fox," he said. "Looks like ole Huckleberry Hound wins. I got ya!"

Charlie and I, in a long off-and-on chase over the years, became known locally as the Hound and the Fox. "I'm gonna put that Fox away forever," he'd boast, but he never did.

He'd won this round, though, and it seemed like a celebration when he brought me into the police station. Other cops shook "Ole Huck's" hand, patted him on the back, treated him like a hero.

I waited seven months in Union County Jail before coming to trial, but it didn't take nearly that long to learn what I faced. They had charged Tony and me with eighty-four robberies, and held the jewelry recovered from his father's house in Virginia as evidence. What really knocked me for a loop was Tony's confession, which they let me read. They also charged Mary with possession of stolen property and suppressing evidence of a felony. The best deal I could make—without implicating Mary—required guilty pleas on four counts.

She never went to jail, nor did Tony. Tony cut his own deal, fed me to the cops, and returned to Virginia on probation while I sat in Union County Jail fuming about getting betrayed by my friend and my girlfriend. I told myself, and meant it at the time, that the worst thing a person could do was care about someone else. In my self-pity, the betrayal by Tony and Mary seemed like another link in a long chain of disappointments.

All that remained was facing Judge Hopkins, known as "The Hanging Judge," in Union County Supreme Court. A guard confided to me, "Keep your eyes open. If the judge adjusts his glasses just before the sentencing, it means you're going to get serious time. That's his signal for the court officers to move in on you."

Well, he moved his glasses and the white shirts started closing in. "Do you have anything to say before I pass sentence?" he asked.

"You've already passed sentence," I said with a smirk, trying to look cool. "Give me my time and get it over with."

Not too smart, but it made me feel good, and strengthened my reputation with tough guys who spread the word about the "kid" who "stood up to" a Supreme Court justice. Too bad my wise mouth was bigger than my brain back then. I should have thrown myself on the mercy of the court, explaining that I'd had a rough ride so far, but I'd determined to do better. Instead I chose to be Mr. Tough Guy and capped the performance by spitting at the judge.

He stuttered, floundered, gave me *ten years,* then instructed the white shirts, "Get this trash out of my court."

I had just turned nineteen when I entered Bordentown, the minimum age this prison would accept. Bordentown was a penitentiary more than a hundred years old, with high walls, steel gates, and dank dungeons they called cells. With the escape from Jamesburg on my record, they assigned me to a maximum security wing, a lockup within a lockup.

Rubbing my shaved head, not yet assigned a job, I lay on a thin mildewed mattress and dreamed of ways to kill Tony Santa. "That double-crosser will pay," I told myself again and again.

A lot of the inmates at Bordentown I remembered from my time at Jamesburg. The two institutions were like schools. You attended "high school" in Jamesburg, where you learned to be a criminal, and then you found yourself in "college" at Bordentown with some of your former classmates. Actually, the time was easier this trip because I had money, and friends I'd known from the past. Most important, there were far fewer rapes and fights now that we had outgrown the Billy the Kid syndrome.

When an incident did occur, however, the consequences were serious. One inmate, a burly homosexual who told the wrong guy, "I'm gonna do you, sweety," was found with a horseshoe imbedded in his head. Someone who didn't pay for cigarettes got stabbed in the heart during a movie. I had a fight with an inmate who lost heavy at cards, couldn't pay, and threatened a friend of mine. I cracked him a few times with two Master No. 5 locks on a web belt, and he woke up in the hospital with twenty-six stitches in his head. His partner, afraid I'd unlock *his* head, paid the debt.

An inmate had to be violent to survive. Let even the slightest insult pass, and life would get very bad for an inmate. Soon he would be somebody's slave or plaything. Fight back, though, show you wouldn't take any abuse, and the animals would move on to easier prey.

The most effective control factor our keepers had was racism. As long as whites and blacks fought one another, there was no danger of a unified protest for change. Inmates automatically segregated themselves into racial groups (blacks far outnumbered everyone else), and the only thing we shared was hatred for the guards. When a riot did break out, it pitted inmate against inmate while the sadistic low IQ hacks looked on with glee. I ended up losing the use of my left hand, tendons cut in three of my fingers. I never ratted on the guy who sent me through the window. He'd already done five years and was about to go home. Besides, I figured I'd catch up with him later.

My only visitor at Bordentown was a girl from Pop Klein's neighborhood who was sweet on me. She served as my eyes and ears to the outside, bringing news about who got busted, married, or killed. Her reports on the activities of my girlfriend Mary particularly held interest for me. I learned Mary was bedding down with some of my "friends," saying I deserved what happened to me, and that she hoped I would never get out. She had sworn eternal love before I went away, and the stories planted murderous thoughts in my head. With the same venom I wished I could get rid of all those who had hurt me, I began to lay plans to hurt Mary.

An inmate could buy booze, drugs, and even women at Bordentown if he could afford it, and a number of the prisoners could. Many had come off spectacular criminal careers, and for others, like me, the "glory days" still lay ahead. Thus, while I was on the countdown to freedom, I worked on making contacts that might be useful in the future. The ten years I'd been given actually meant two, if I kept my nose clean, and I calculated my release date was not many months off.

Wrong. With just sixty days to go, a guard named Wholey came to my cell before breakfast and said, "Get dressed, Minucci. You're going to court."

"What for? There's gotta be a mistake."

"Get yourself dressed. There's no mistake. The papers just came down."

I found out what he was talking about in a holding room at the Middlesex County Supreme Court, from a court-appointed lawyer. The cops had evidence about another burglary I'd participated in, and intended to nail me for it.

"Plead guilty," the court-appointed lawyer advised. "The worst you'll get is a concurrent sentence."

Figuring this mouthpiece knew what he was talking about, I went into the courtroom. The judge gave me ten years to run *consecutive* with the previous term.

"I'm really hurt by this," the young lawyer said, uttering one of the most unbelievable sentences I've ever heard. "They didn't treat me right."

Treat *him* right? I wanted to wrap my hands around his neck. Oddly enough, I viewed the situation as one where once again I'd foolishly trusted someone, and been betrayed. The time was coming when, dangerous and paranoid, I refused to trust anyone.

Two years later I walked out of Bordentown, the words of a captain named Stickles ringing in my ears: "You'll be back in thirty days."

I never saw the inside of Bordentown again, nor any other prison for more than a month. I would be questioned and charged with many crimes—bookmaking, extortion, hijacking, armed robbery, attempted murder—but none of it stuck and they always cut me loose.

Several police departments set up betting pools with the cash going to the officer who could bag me and send me away for more than a year.

It's not something to be proud of, but the fact is, no one ever collected that money.

Chapter 3

What happened next was really not something to be proud of, but by this time I had turned into a savage. "I want Mary dead," I told Petie, a young shooter I'd met at Bordentown.

"It will cost you a thousand," he said.

"Half up front." I handed him five hundred.

"Let me know when and where."

I called Mary. "Frankie!" she said. "It's been a long time. I've waited for you, just like I promised. I'm sorry I didn't visit, but with work and all . . ."

"Forget it. I know how busy you've been. Let's celebrate. Get dolled up and meet me at the Rahway train station tomorrow night at nine. In the tunnel by the newsstand. We'll paint the town red."

Blood red, I thought, my bitterness and hatred making human feelings impossible.

The train station, I knew, figured to be deserted at 9 P.M., and any witness could alibi me out of the murder: "Officer, I saw this young man talking to the girl when a gunman darted out of the shadows and shot her. It was just awful."

I actually envied Petie's task and felt shortchanged at not having the pleasure of squeezing the trigger myself. But this way was better. I could settle the score without jeopardizing my freedom.

Mary showed up promptly at nine in the underground walkway,

flashing a slightly forced smile and throwing her arms around my neck. "Frankie," she said, "it's so good to have you back."

Detecting no response from my statue stillness, she took a step backward, and Petie was behind her, the gun barrel pressing against her skull.

"Don't turn around," he said, in that flat tone used by cops and gangsters.

"Frankie . . ."

I felt a deadening *satisfaction*. Alone in the dim light, I had time to tell her *why* she was going to die.

"Payback time," I growled, my voice filled with venom and menace. "Getting even was all I thought about for three long years."

Here's the kind of person I'd become: I waited for her to deny giving me up and being unfaithful, to cry for forgiveness and beg for mercy, before the planned-for denouement: watching her die with a lie on her lips, the hatred in my eyes the last thing she saw.

But there were no tears, no pleas. Mary began shaking. Her legs buckled under my death stare and she crumpled to her knees, trembling pathetically, a skinny ninety-pound waif crying for her mommie.

Suddenly it wasn't at all the dramatic scene I had dreamt a thousand times. Shooting her would be like destroying a whimpering pitiful animal. The words came out without willing them. "Get lost," I said to Petie. "We'll pass on this one."

Like most hitmen, no matter how vigorously they deny it, Petie *enjoyed* killing. He had come here psyched up, similar to a football player prepared for a big game, and now, unfulfilled, needed to bring himself down. Maybe it was more basic: a kid promised candy and then told he couldn't have it. Petie tensed, fumed, glared as if considering turning the gun on me.

"You ain't gettin' your money back," he managed to say. He spit on the kneeling Mary and stalked away.

What to do with my ex-girlfriend? All I could think of was to curse her, then, not satisfied, I kicked her in the stomach—"This is your lucky day"—and left her writhing on the concrete.

★   ★   ★

Armed with solid gold recommendations from wiseguys I'd befriended at Bordentown, I started hanging out in Newark nightclubs owned by people in organized crime: Johnny Morris, Vinnie Lubianco, Roy Hardin, Eddie Madden. Also, Ira Pesnick, a prolific killer and so-called tough guy, who ratted out a lot of the Campisi crew after he got busted.

Soon I was working for some of these guys: taking numbers, hijacking trucks, breaking legs.

And partying. I couldn't get enough of the easy life. What we called "work"—the drinking and carousing to make contacts in these nightclubs—is today sometimes called "networking." On one of these nightly binges I met Frankie Famular, who went by "Frankie Fame," and we became fast friends. A talent agent whose company represented local entertainers, Fame gave himself top billing. He'd appeared in *On the Waterfront* with Marlon Brando, but mainly he was a world-class drummer. He played with the Glenn Miller Band, Buddy Rich, Gene Krupa; and the jazz from his own five-piece combo rivaled New Orleans' best. Of course, Fame knew all the wiseguys, and his recommendation to mob bigshot Rocky Stango led to an okay for opening my own joint.

I packed the place with go-go girls who doubled up hustling drinks, and soon was pulling down $1,500 a week from the operation. Most guys my age, twenty-two, made a tenth of that, if lucky. And they didn't have their pick of lively dancers to bed down after the music stopped. Borrowing a page from Fame's book, I formed an agency for young "talent" willing to bare all and hawk watered-down cocktails, positions the mob clubs always had open.

Lucky in business, unlucky at love, I resumed what had to rank as one of history's sickest relationships—with Mary. *She* came to me, and I took her back. We were an item, but not really tight; she continued sleeping with my friends, and anyone else available, while I had that stable of go-go girls.

Our rocky relationship rocked on until 1964 when, in front of a Rahway justice of the peace, I vowed to love, honor, and cherish a woman I didn't even *like*, one I hated for having betrayed me. Why did I do it? Because she was pregnant—like father, like son.

Looking back more than thirty years, I'd say the marriage was an unmitigated disaster—fights all the time, adulterous affairs on both sides that would require a small telephone-size book to list.

But I can't say that. The on/mostly-off union produced four children, all now grown—Ronald, Jay, Candice, Keith—and I pray they accomplish all the positive things their parents didn't.

I don't need to dwell on Mary's shortcomings. Back then she was what people called white trash, and I wasn't any better— worse, in fact. I was a great provider—whatever they needed, I stole—but a lousy father and a thoroughly unloving husband. Except for delivering money, I preferred to be an absentee head of household.

I can't say I was unhappy those few years in the nightclub business, doing jobs on the side, but life seemed *too tame.* In the thick of murders—a lot of guys were getting hit—and scams, ripoffs, armed heists, extortion, payoffs, paybacks, all forms of criminal madness, I still yearned for something more exciting. The mobsters I knew were professional well-dressed criminals who spent every waking moment scheming, putting in almost twice the hours of a legitimate job, to earn a fat living illegally. But after a while I got bored, and all the underworld glitz took on the dullness of a night at Pop Klein's house.

I had met a few outlaw bikers, members of the Pagans, and grew fascinated by their freewheeling lifestyle—sex, drugs, in-your-face violence. Gradually these shirtless renegades looked more attractive than the white collar, ever-serious wiseguys I worked for. I wasn't cut out to be a businessman and hated having to, on occasion, play Mr. Two Face. Bikers who didn't like you let you know it up front. They would put a boot on your neck and make you watch them rape your wife. Sad to say, at that point in my life, the biker world drew me in.

They were losers, all of them, but you could count on them for backing no matter the right or wrong. They didn't have to seek approval from anybody to avenge an insult, and the cops feared them more than the Mafia.

A bunch of us, in April 1965, decided to form our own outlaw club, the Nomads. We knew about a group with the same name in Arizona, so we changed the colors and designed a flying death head as our logo. Charter members included Shades, Suds, Undertaker, Daffy, Cyclops, PeeWee, and Ginzo. On our debut night as Nomads, we swaggered into a bar, picked a fight with some wannabe bikers, and then said we'd let PeeWee, all five feet of him, fight the three of them by himself.

"You gonna throw the baby at us?" sneered one of the wannabes.

"Don't hurt me too bad," said PeeWee.

It took thirty seconds for our karate brother to flatten the three men, who wound up leaving in an ambulance.

My biker years—and this is saying something—were the lowest, dirtiest, and meanest of my life. I don't know if an abomination existed that I didn't stand ready to commit. I grew a beard, mustache, and hair down to my belt; wore the same dungarees for months. I wasn't voted president by the brothers because of my sweet disposition. There were shootings, rapes, robberies, arson, torture, drug dealing, and Satanism.

Money didn't matter much. All we needed was enough to keep the party going. One night Cyclops and I robbed the house of my former best friend Frankie Fame; all he did was bawl me out and say I ought to examine my life.

It seemed everyone wanted to be a biker; clubs popped up all over the country. A few were cool. Most couldn't cut it. The clubs had names like Bandanas, Breed, Wheels, Iron Cross, East Bay Dragons, Comancheros, Trotters, Pagans, and of course, the Hell's Angels. At first we partied together, but reputation became important and then wars broke out. Biker clubs responded to slights, real or imagined, with beatings, torture, even murder.

A lot of guys died; many more went to prison. Clashes with police became frequent and occasionally deadly. Bars and businesses got wrecked and burned over minor differences. Everybody had a gun.

We operated under strange rules that made us different from the rest of the world. For example, a Nomad who fell asleep or passed out during a party was doused with gasoline and set on fire. I did it to a guy named Bones and scarred him for life.

I lived my biker years totally out of control. Everyone feared me. I loved the fact that kids saw me as a role model, girls wanted me as their steady, other up-and-coming biker clubs put a price on my head, and the Rahway police training classes used me as an example of the ultimate bad guy to rookies.

We ravaged a town in New York state after a local businessman sold all-the-beer-you-can-drink tickets and then put out a single keg. Another time, when one of the brothers got fired from his job at a local laundry for "borrowing" a company truck to transport beer on one of our runs, we made a bonfire in the parking lot from all the cleaned clothing, trashed the building, and disabled every delivery truck.

When we weren't grossing out citizens—riding through sedate downtown streets mooning housewives and shop owners—we fought turf wars with other clubs; consumed gargantuan amounts of drugs, beer, and whisky; and challenged police to arrest us for blatant traffic violations. The cops stayed out of that game, but the biker wars heated up. The widely held view, shared by the Nomads, was that the East Coast had room for only one outlaw club. It was not unlike cutthroat business competition, I suppose. Make no mistake, there were biker leaders who saw ways to profit, especially in the drug market, where competition is always fierce.

I had long stopped associating with traditional mobsters, the flashy Machiavellian think-alikes in suits, and lived full-time as an independent Nomad. However, the bodies were piling up, and when the Hell's Angels, dipping their toes in Eastern waters, proposed a get-together of all the clubs, the Nomads agreed to attend. The date was set—Labor Day weekend, 1967—and the gathering finally ended up in a park thirty miles outside Lancaster, Pennsylvania.

After several run-ins with the law, we assembled by clubs and traveled two-by-two behind state trooper cars to a park thirty miles away. The line of bikes stretched *two miles*, probably the largest collection of outlaws ever to ride together.

A large but remote section of the park had been blocked off for us, and the police disappeared. I didn't doubt they lurked just out of sight, but we'd have no more confrontations with them this weekend.

Amid the craziness—everyone drunk or doped to the max, fighting, women passed around—the Hell's Angels told the various club presidents what they had in mind.

I got the word from a nasty-looking outlaw, as wide as he was tall with a monumental beer gut, who said he spoke for Sonny Barger, Angels leader himself. "The Pagans are righteous brothers," he told me. "Sonny wants them to form an East Coast branch of the Angels. Only the classiest outlaws from any club, including the Pagans, will be welcome."

"All the Nomads got class," I said. "They're all eligible."

"We'll see."

"I ain't abandonin' no brothers."

It turned out my objections were a minor glitch compared to those encountered elsewhere. The Pagans themselves were for the idea, but they refused to replace their pagan god logo with the flying death head made famous by the Californians. The Angels tried to compromise, saying the pagan god could be worn upside down underneath the Angel logo.

The Pagans considered this an insult, as they should have. The Angels more than anyone should have known how important the colors are to an outlaw. They symbolize the deepest form of friendship and brotherhood.

Within a few weeks a war broke out between the Pagans and Hell's Angels, and a lot of clubs got caught in between, a war that has continued for twenty-eight years, right up to the present. Hundreds have died.

At first a small number of Hell's Angels came from the West Coast and leased a building on New York City's Lower East Side. They lived and recruited from there, one member at a time, slowly, carefully, but any outlaw biker would have to be really stupid not to recognize the threat they posed.

Knowing numbers would be important, I helped merge the Nomads with the Aliens and Comancheros to form the Aliens/Nomads and was elected president.

The major problem was defections. The Hell's Angels had the reputation, and a number of our outlaws crossed over.

Killings increased dramatically. Wearing the "wrong" colors became sufficient reason to torture and murder a rival. I saw it firsthand.

One evening in late 1967 I visited a brother named Shoe who lived in a beach bungalow on the southeastern tip of Staten Island. At 10 P.M. we were smoking grass when the doorbell rang. Shoe went to answer, his two sons—ages four and six—right behind him. He opened the door and outlaws with shotguns blew his head off.

I scrambled behind the couch, drawing my .25 automatic, blood and bits of brain dripping from my clothes and face. But the killers vanished into the night. The next thing I knew, Sheila, Shoe's wife, was screaming and pounding her head on the floor.

I stayed around till the cops questioned me, till the meat wagon took Shoe's body away, till Sheila could remove herself and the kids to her mother's home. Oddly enough, my first thoughts weren't of revenge, but about the tragic madness of our lives.

Later, sitting on my bed in Rahway, the colors at my feet, spattered with Shoe's blood, my mind filled with negatives. Too many brothers had died, and many more rotted in jail. The cops had begun to infiltrate the clubs, with devastating results. One man-and-woman team brought down *ninety-one* bikers. To get close enough to the brothers, the male cop became a stone-cold doper; the woman had to sleep with anyone who wanted her.

A number of factors influenced my decision to leave the biker life, but right at the top was what I saw happen to Shoe. I also sensed the Hell's Angels represented the wave of the future, and with them it would never be the same. We'd be small cogs in a big wheel.

I announced my resignation at the next Aliens/Nomads meeting. Guys yelled and cursed, urged me to stay, but I told them I couldn't. It could have gotten ugly, but they knew I told the truth when I wished them well and said I loved them. They were all outcasts, just like me, and I felt for them.

It was April 1968, and I needed to figure out what to do with the rest of my life. Serving God didn't enter the equation, though strangely enough the "experience" I was gathering would help me understand "lost" souls to whom I later ministered. More important, I think, my life would prove that if there were hope for me, there was hope for anyone.

Chapter 4

Big Daddy Von Emery, my former biker brother, had a nose for business, a knack for recognizing profit-making opportunities which, though right in front of you, might go unnoticed in the hustle of everyday life. Just after I left the Nomads, he came to me with a get-rich-quick idea.

"We've been missing our calling," he said. "We need to get with it. Become part of the scene."

"What are you talking about?"

"We need to join the hippie culture."

"That's crazy," I said.

"Think about it. What do hippies do?"

"They protest. Have sex. Use drugs."

"Repeat that last."

"They use drugs."

"Exactly. *Lots* of drugs. Our job will be to make sure they have all they want."

"It could be a money-maker," I judged. No other thought entered my head.

"The deal can't miss. It's perfect, I tell you. It will be as easy as shearing sheep."

Big Daddy had it all worked out. We would drive our customized camper we'd put together to Manhattan's East Village and set up shop: literally, a street corner drugstore. Our biker connections meant supply would be no problem.

The camper was a sight. "Groovy" and "far out," the street people called it. Bright white with bold gold stripes, it was the equivalent of a modern Winnebago motorhome. Big Daddy and I were really proud of the RV we'd constructed from a pair of stolen bread trucks, cutting the back off one, the nose off another, and welding them together. The 28-foot-long vehicle needed three drive shafts and a big Caddy engine. A gas-powered generator provided electricity, heat, and air-conditioning to an interior we'd finished out to two bedrooms, living room, kitchen, bathroom, and furnished with sofas, easy chairs, coffee tables, TV/stereo, plus numerous rollaway cots for crashing.

Low overhead also made the venture attractive. No rent payments or long-term lease for us. We simply parked the motorhome on Second Avenue near St. Mark's Place (it occupied three spaces) and there it largely remained for 2½ years, eventually becoming a Village landmark. The cops never bothered us. Not once.

Why? It was the times. The police had enough hassles trying to keep the lid on a potentially explosive social situation without making an insignificant drug bust.

I adopted the name "Lee." Big Daddy dropped the "Big" for the more user-friendly "Daddy." Real head-knockers in our recent biker days, we traded our colors for love beads, cowboy boots, guitars, and pot pipes.

It didn't take long to learn the lingo: the rich comprised the Establishment, much hated; military officers were fascists; the cops were pigs and porkers. Among themselves, however, Village denizens talked about peace, love, and sharing. In other words, a perfect situation for a pair of wolves like Von Emery and me.

Since many of the hippies had no money, we often operated a trading post, exchanging drugs, mostly speed and pot, for radios, cameras, and other goods lifted from tourists, or jewelry that runaways had "liberated" from their parents. When the motorhome overflowed with merchandise, we transported it to the largest flea market on the East Coast, in Englishtown, New Jersey, and then dickered with bargain-hunting suburbanites.

Girls were everywhere and the pickings easy, especially if you stood against the war in Vietnam. I suppose I did; even a tough hide like mine couldn't help being softened by the earnest arguments of these committed young people. However, if you weren't opposed to the war, you needed to pretend you were. The kids, no matter how desperate for drugs, wouldn't do business otherwise.

The Village was the place to be in the late sixties, colorful and bristling with the activity of a new generation determined to change the world. Besides, I loved music, and here I was, right in the music capitol of the world, able to walk down the street or gaze out a window of the motorhome and see many of the rock-and-roll greats. It was even better for Daddy and me. Some of the musicians—legends or legends-to-be—used our camper as a resting place to chill out for a while and escape from the frenetic activity surrounding them. Jimi Hendrix, performing at world-famous Fillmore East, just a stone's throw from our curbside homestead, dropped in between acts.

"Man, you got the best speed in the world," he always said, lounging in an overstuffed chair.

Bob Dylan was another who regularly stopped by to escape the crowd and enjoy a joint and some red wine. Mostly he came to talk about motorcycles. He had owned a Harley as a teenager in Minnesota, and even a terrible 1967 bike crash in upstate New York, which put his career on hold for almost four years, didn't dim his enthusiasm for the big hogs.

The yippie leaders Abbie Hoffman and Jerry Rubin stopped by on several occasions, covered head-to-foot with protest buttons. Of the two, I preferred Abbie. Always talking and laughing, he agreed with Jimi Hendrix that we dealt the world's best speed. I told Abbie motorcycle stories, tales of incredible parties and violent rumbles, and he wanted to bet that he had more scars to show for his lifestyle than I did. The truth is, he had plenty. His head was a target the cops loved.

I owned a Martin (the Rolls-Royce of guitars) I'd bought for $300 from a root beer stand owner. One afternoon, strumming it in the passenger seat of the camper (playing "Pilgrim"), a guy looked in the open window.

"Would you like to hear the real version of that?" he asked.

"Yes, sure!" I said, recognizing one of my favorite singers, Kris Kristofferson.

Daddy and I conducted Kristofferson and two of his friends on a tour of the motorhome, then he sat down, accepted a beer, and swallowed a pill he removed from a small rosewood box he carried. When he left, an hour later, he forgot the box. I still have it.

Our former biker brothers visited occasionally, and we were happy to see them. It was cool unless one of the hippies called them "greasers," in which case the hippie got stomped. Guys like Undertaker and Cyclops stood out even in Greenwich Village psychedelia.

Our drug business took care of itself. We were open for business twenty-four hours a day. It didn't matter to us, cash or trade.

For our part, Daddy and I were living on methamphetamines and hardly ever sleeping. We had been using the stuff since our biker days and had become half-crazy. The more wild and vicious we became, the more customers began staying away.

Devils and demons bathed in flames began to paint record album covers, and when Daddy suggested we adopt the Marquis de Sade as our role model, I only raised an eyebrow to ask, "Who's he?"

"Some French guy. Lived two hundred years ago. Sadism's named for him."

"Yeah? What's that mean to us?"

It meant, I soon learned, bondage and submission for the many females unlucky enough to fall into our trap. Village girls who considered it an honor to be invited into our "groovy" motorhome were sucked in and victimized. We degraded more young women than I care to recount.

I teetered on the brink of self-destruction, and Daddy, his arms zigzagged with needle tracks, wandered permanently out in orbit.

Then he brought Bella into our lives. She had long raven hair, large brown eyes, creamy white skin—an Elvira lookalike. I asked her what she did.

"I'm a witch," she replied.

Daddy was wild in love with his new woman, and before long asked her to move into the motorhome. She arrived with a satchel full of books about curses, charms, and spells, plus a huge, white, golden-eyed Belgian shepherd chained to her wrist. The dog, Lucifer, served as her pet and protector. I thought I was on a bad trip the first time I heard her chanting praises to the devil.

A few of us, as bikers, had dabbled in the occult, but the deepest we got was attending a black mass that we judged as nonsense. Bella couldn't be dismissed so easily. She talked fervently and constantly about the powers of witchcraft, witches, and especially Satan. Twenty-four years old, she headed a coven of a dozen men and women who survived by begging and stealing. Often they wore plastic skulls and what at first I *thought* were imitation animal parts purchased at one of the Village's spooky occult shops. It's what I thought, that is, until Daddy insisted I accompany Bella and her coven to a cemetery. They sacrificed several dogs and cats, daubed one another with blood, and cavorted on freshly dug graves to summon the deceased from hell.

"Get her out," I told Daddy one day when she'd slipped out to browse in an occult shop.

"Are you crazy? Bella possesses great powers. We can have those same powers." He stopped to inject himself in an exceedingly hard-to-find vein. "Besides, I'm in love with her. She's in love with me."

When Bella and I were alone, she often came on to me. I suspected her recruitment of male coven members began exactly this way. Probably the women, too. Outwardly Bella qualified as a knockout, a ten, perfect except for her too-pale skin, but her weird, sick behavior and practices quenched any ardor I might otherwise have felt.

"Do you like my new candles?" she asked one night when Daddy was out.

"I prefer the lightbulbs we used to burn."

"But these candles are special. They're made from the fat tissue of a baby I sacrificed last night."

I had no way of knowing whether she told the truth. My mind, recoiling from what she'd said, refused to believe her. A little part of me, though, wasn't so sure. "Why don't you get yourself out of our lives?" I shouted.

Lucifer bristled and drew a golden-eyed bead on me. Usually very well behaved, he would rip the throat out of anyone threatening his mistress.

"I want you in my coven," Bella said.

"I should kill you," I said. The thought had crossed my mind.

"Don't be silly. You and I have a future. Daddy's too far gone with drugs. You're still strong. Together we'll have power *and* money."

Daddy was definitely too far gone, but I stood close behind. I felt as if I resided in the Land of Oz, but no one would mistake me for the lovable Tin Man. The ups had turned me into a snarling monster. Longtime hippie customers coming for marijuana and speed from the former biker-turned-cool-dude now encountered Wolfman under a full moon.

Still, I wasn't far enough gone to consider Bella's offer. Although she drank moderate amounts of wine and smoked a potent blend of hash to show she belonged, there was more evil to this high witch than met the eye. She called her female followers "sisters" and "children," sent them out with instructions to use sex to recruit—Hookers for Satan—and always showed up at the end of the day to collect the money. Her male followers were airheads, programmed dummies who stole on command and delivered the loot to Bella, who *half*-believed in Satanism and one hundred percent in "free enterprise." Bella had not yet become rich, but the potential was there.

The saddest, most distorted subject in this unreal picture was Big Daddy Von Emery, the once strapping, fear-inspiring hulk, reduced to a pathetic tribute to Bella's wiles. Daddy actually crawled around on all fours, wearing a collar and chain, begging the high witch to whip him.

Why didn't I leave?

I should have, but the motorhome was half mine, and I thought I'd be a fool to let Bella have it. I turned ways to get rid of her over and over in my mind.

One night, Daddy was away on some make-work errand for

Bella. A terrific thunderstorm and howling wind rocked the sturdy camper. The rain fell in sheets on the deserted streets of Iselin, New Jersey, where we had parked the RV for the weekend. Lightning and burning candles provided the only flickering illumination. Even devil dog, lips curled, lay whimpering under a table, frightened by the thunder and rain pounding like bullets on the roof.

I'd been lying on my bed, watching lightning reflect on the walls. Suddenly Bella was beside me.

For an instant I was tempted. Then I remembered how I'd felt when I learned in prison that Mary had been sleeping with my friends.

Somehow she read my mind. "Daddy will never know," she whispered.

I shoved her hard and she went sailing out of the bed onto the floor. "Lucifer, get him!" she said.

The ghostly white dog flew out from under the table, growling low, fangs bared, hair standing up on its back. My left hand automatically cupped my crotch—I knew that's where the dog would aim—and I spun away from the beast to lay my right hand on the .38 revolver I kept on a shelf over the bed. Lucifer thumped me full force in the back as I gripped the gun.

Sprawled facedown on the bed, I heard Bella hiss, "Kill him! Kill him, boy!"

He was trying and would have succeeded if I hadn't twisted around, grabbed a handful of blanket, and stuffed it between his jaws. The last thought I had before shooting him three times in the head was how strong this animal was.

Blood had spattered cabinets and walls. Bella crawled to the beast's side, trembling and crying. I knelt next to her, pointed the gun at her head, and squeezed the trigger. But I had purposefully aimed a few inches high and the bullet slammed into a cabinet.

Bella stared at me with eyes as blank as her dog's, then curled into a fetal position and lay nearly still on the floor. Playing out another incredibly low point in my brutish life, I grabbed her by the hair and yanked her face close to mine. "I'm leaving for the night," I said. "I'll put a bullet in your head if you're here in the morning."

I carried and dragged the dog through the rain and wind to

the nearby river and dumped him in the dark water, then trudged back to an abandoned Sinclair gas station that once was our biker headquarters, where I spent the night. The next morning, with a friend along to cover my back in case she had a gun or had summoned her broom-flying friends, I returned home.

Bella had left, but Daddy was there, beside himself with rage and grief. "You killed her, didn't you?" he yelled.

"Daddy, I didn't kill her. I swear. Sit down and I'll tell you what happened."

"You shot her! I can prove it! You were jealous of us and you shot her!"

We had gone inside and he gestured at the bloodstains on the bed, carpet, and walls—so much blood—and pointed at the bullet hole in the cabinet.

"She's not dead, Daddy. Let me—"

"She wouldn't give you the time of day, would she? That's what set you off. She loved me and you couldn't have her. You had it all planned, didn't you? That's why you sent me away. Soon as I left, you whacked her."

"*She* sent you away. Think, Daddy! It was her!"

Big Daddy didn't want to think. Believing his life's love was lost and nothing could ever replace her, he refused to listen to anything I said.

Instead of directing his anger and hatred outward toward me, he directed it inward. I didn't think it possible, but he increased the frequency of the meth shots. Daddy rarely spoke, except to ask, "Where did you bury her body?" and "Did you rape Bella before you killed her?"

The very real danger existed that he would try to kill me. I knew I'd defend myself, but I had no heart for that. Daddy had been a good friend once. But even though the drugs had changed him, taking his life, albeit in self-defense, held no honor for me.

In the end, the motorhome hardly left the Sinclair station. Daddy never washed or changed clothes, and greeted the few who knocked on the back door with curses and threats. We stayed doped up the whole time.

After one of my infrequent food runs, I returned to find Daddy had barricaded himself inside. When I beat on the door, he said, "I ain't lyin'. I'll kill you if you don't go away."

That's how I left him, in August 1970, a madman locked in a box on wheels.

Chapter 5

I moved Mary and the four children we'd produced from her mother's home to a house I rented for them near Linden, New Jersey, and continued my drug dealing from there. I kept about 500 keys of pot in the basement and thousands of hits of blotter acid in the freezer. Mainly my customers were bikers, but once a week I'd go to the Village and the hippie crowd that counted on me, plus I'd established a new clientele through word-of-mouth.

The problem was, I'd become my own best customer. Speed had me hooked big-time and was sure to reel me in sooner than later. A dealer needed to be smart, but the drugs made me stupid. Stupidity combined with biker recklessness made me an easy target for cops.

"Frankie," said Blackie Zeal, a guy I considered a friend. "You got a death wish? If you do, it's gonna get granted. You're more wasted than your customers."

Blackie, a knockaround guy with good connections, had a reputation for doing stickups and break-ins. The building didn't exist that he couldn't bust into. He had been a long haul truck driver in earlier days and knew about being wired on meth.

"Let me help you," he said.

"How you plan to do that?" Like most junkies, I wanted help;

and then again, I didn't. Life without dope did not seem worthwhile. Life with it, though, promised to be short and painful.

"Trust me."

Blackie, fifteen years older than me, stood a stocky five-feet-six, 170 pounds. He fancied he knew a little about being a doctor, but the one time he practiced medicine (on himself) hardly inspired confidence. He'd been in a bar drinking with a friend, who noticed Blackie's infected right index finger had turned black.

"You got gangrene," the friend observed. "That finger will have to go before the gangrene spreads."

"You're right." Blackie quickly downed half-a-dozen shots of vodka, stuck the finger in his mouth, and bit off about a half-inch of it.

Blackie and his wife Barbara were both very superstitious, another quality I didn't think would help whatever drug therapy he had planned for me. But, I shrugged, if it works . . .

Barbara once had a premonition of something bad happening during an upcoming resort robbery, and wouldn't let Blackie accompany his four partners. While the stickup came down—a hundred or so guests herded into a circle, ordered to hand over their valuables—one of the gang discovered a guest holding back, became enraged, and nearly cut the man in half with machine gun fire. All four of those guys got life sentences. The cops work a lot harder on crimes when a death occurs. Probably there would have been no arrests if that hothead hadn't opened fire.

Blackie's own criminal career, he said, started after he got fired as a teenager from his job in a funeral home. Even today (he's still a friend of mine) he thinks getting canned was unjust. What he did was substitute his body for a corpse, and pop out of the coffin in front of startled relatives as they prepared to view the departed.

Anyway, I agreed to Blackie's help with my drug problem, and we drove to his home in an isolated spot near Linden. Blackie and Barbara led me into their backyard, sat me in a chair, and made ready to strap me down.

"What's going on?" I bellowed.

"We're saving your life," said Barbara Zeal softly. "You'll only be tied up a short time."

"How short?"

"Not long at all."

"How long is 'not long'?"

"Seventy-two hours."

Each hour was the length of a year.

Most of the time I spent alone, except for a huge brown dog named Scotty who stood guard in case I got loose.

The sweat came first, popping out all over my body, acrid foul-smelling stuff that made me constrict my throat and clamp my jaws tight to hold back the vomit. The odor was awful, sickly, sour; my skin, drenched in poisonous liquid, soaked my clothes and left me squirming in puddles of my own fluid.

"Blackie!" I called out, at first employing a reasonable tone. "Barbara! Come out here, please! I need to see you!" But no one came, and my tone changed. I switched to obscenities, then threats, but only that big, placid brown dog seemed to hear.

It was hot under a high August sun, but I shivered as though naked in the Yukon. Cold, clammy, fat drops of sweat made maddening treks from my armpits down my sides to hips and beyond. The straps had been fastened so tightly I could barely wriggle.

I threw up, one mighty barf that caked my torso and even my legs to the knees. All the junk I'd ingested for a decade, now rancid, seemed to regurgitate in a stink a hundred times worse than the sweat.

Suddenly Blackie was in front of me, holding something long and thin I couldn't identify. I tried to speak, my mind a murky confused mix of hatred and despair, but whatever might have come out got washed away by water spewing from the hose he held. He drenched me front and back, top to bottom. Poorly formed thoughts that he'd release me long enough to change clothes drifted in and out of my mind, along with an idea that I'd overpower him—really make him pay for all this—but he took no chances. I don't remember his saying a word. He walked back to the house and closed the back door behind him.

Next came the hallucinations: snakes, grinning skulls pushing out of the ground—evil, rotting skulls, death's-heads staring at me through hollow sockets, then turning toward the holes from which they'd emerged, an invitation for me to join. Terror taunted me the entire first night, broken only briefly (at what time I don't know) by Barbara appearing at my side and somehow coaxing me to eat a small bowl of soup.

Discomfort and mental suffering were replaced the second day by searing physical pain: terrific headaches and lightning bolts shooting through my joints, rockets of hurt that would have propelled me bolt upright—if I'd been able to move. The severity of the agony seldom varied, but my reactions did. Alternately I whimpered, screamed, or prayed for death. I cursed the big brown dog, though the expression in his eyes was the closest I've ever witnessed to pure compassion.

Three times this second day Barbara came to feed me. "You're doing good, Frankie," she said. "You're doing fine. Blackie and I are proud of you."

But she wouldn't release the straps, no matter how pitifully I pled or realistically threatened.

I called her names and she was saving my life.

Paranoia ruled the third day. I looked like a wild animal. Thought like one, too. What motives did Blackie and Barbara harbor? I imagined they plotted to take over my drug business. Or maybe they had been hired to kill me slowly, by someone nursing a special, intense hatred. I knew of such murders, but none carried out quite like this one.

Was I being poisoned? Perhaps that's why I'd experienced so much pain, why my mind played tricks on me with the snakes and skulls. I refused to eat when Barbara brought food. Most of the time I lolled half-awake, half-asleep, my thoughts listless and vaguely formed. The brown dog nestled at my feet.

The morning after my third night in the backyard, Blackie and Barbara unstrapped me, carried me into the house, and laid me on a crisp, freshly made bed. Something good had happened, but I didn't know what. I stretched out and slept, waking six or seven times for a few minutes, around the clock for forty-eight hours.

I awakened for good, weak and in a daze but feeling clean— more accurately, cleaned out. Actually, I was filthy, "something the cat dragged in," Barbara said, but clean *inside*. After a long shower, wearing a robe Blackie bought for me, I listened to them saying how proud I should be. What happened, of course, I'd gone through the equivalent of detox and cold-turkeyed a monster addiction to speed.

I let them praise me, but all credit belonged to them. They had forced me—no other way existed—to save my own life. I thanked them before driving home that evening, and have repeated the thanks many times since.

Blackie and I still had many adventures waiting for us, a few quite profitable. For some reason, however, we more often produced results that could be expected from Ralph Kramden and Ed Norton. We committed some monumental boners.

Once we stole what we thought was $300,000 in silver bars, only to learn it was pewter. Another time, on a tip from Blackie's nephew that a certain landlord kept $15,000 cash in a closet of his home, we staked the guy's house out for a month. It seemed he *never* went outside. We were parked outside so long that neighborhood Mafiosi thought we were cops. It got so we had invested so much time in the surveillance that we felt we couldn't break it off. At last the guy left, and we were inside in two seconds. For ninety minutes we tore the place apart, starting with the closet, and here's exactly what we walked out with: a hat, a broken watch, and a nickel.

Giving the nephew who tipped us onto this score the beating of his life was a task we embraced with vigor and enthusiasm.

We missed a couple scores because of Blackie's superstitions. Once it was a black cat crossing his path; another time an old lady said hello to him, which he interpreted as a hex.

Anyway, I had kicked a drug habit, but not drugs. Selling junk remained the quickest method I knew to accumulate possessions and acquire an all-important sense of security. I equated money and *things* with well-being and set out with a passion to become enormously rich. Nobody could hurt you if you were rich, I reasoned. It didn't occur to me what I'd do if I attained my goal. Lots of guys I met dreamed of the "big score" and retirement to Florida or some other sunny clime, but I never planned that far ahead. Even murky, sketchily formed visions of the future were foreign to me.

To make my act more professional, I bought an expensive wardrobe and a smooth-running 1968 Pontiac GTO. All well and good for a guy on the way up, as I imagined myself to be, but I hadn't left my biker and hippie personas totally behind. I also purchased a van with Porky Pig painted on the side. Porky wore a cop's uniform and had his middle finger stuck in the air. Very showy, and not too wise for someone in my line of business, but it depicted what I thought of authority and impressed my Village hippie friends. I might as well have been carrying a sign saying ARREST ME, but the police left me alone. Maybe they figured that anyone this brazen had to be clean.

Early in 1971 I started collecting for some loansharks in Elizabeth, and combined with dealing drugs, plus storing large stashes in my home, I was pulling in $1,000 a week, no sweat. The kids had everything except what they needed most, an at-home, role-model father. My wife followed her own lights. She had more boyfriends than my mother, but I came not to care.

Christmas, in terms of presents, occurred about once a week at the Minucci home. Blackie Zeal and I would cruise the better neighborhoods late at night in the Porky Pig van, grabbing bikes, hot wheel trikes, swing sets, and the like, surprising our kids the next morning. Each of us could have afforded to buy the stuff, but we deemed shopping a "hassle." It was easier to steal.

A weird collection of people gathered around me, and my obsession with material possessions seemed to contradict my easy-come, easy-go attitude toward money. If a friend needed help, he could get it from me. Wiseguys I knew were amazed. I had a reputation as a fierce collector—willing to hurt a luckless debtor—but with my own money ranked as a soft touch.

The guys I hung out with included superflies, burned-out hippies, mind-numbed Vietnam vets, washed-up bikers, disillusioned radicals, greasers left over from the fifties, people still wearing faded, forgotten Nehru jackets—all of them, like myself, trying to figure out who they were. I'm a friend of these people today, and they still don't know. Maybe it's the changed biker scene, or the lack of a Vietnam to spark them, but no one's made a move in more than two decades.

My entourage provided security, eyes and ears on the street for information I couldn't have collected myself. It seemed everyone was into drugs, especially marijuana, and I knew competition would turn nasty.

The easiest way to eliminate a competitor involved hiding a few ounces of pot in his car, scattering some pills around, then calling the police as a concerned citizen and providing a license plate number. The cops, particularly in Rahway, became positively rabid when they busted someone carrying even a single joint. A few ounces guaranteed a sentence of six months to a year.

As turf wars increased, so did the level of ferocity. A lot of dealers, myself included, refused to be branded as rats and took a more direct approach to the problem of competition. Like a personally delivered "Move on, Fool, or else" message, and if that didn't work, their cars or homes might get shotgunned. Something was terribly wrong with this life, and it should have been obvious to me, but it wasn't.

Happy Jack, a former biker in the Nomads, lent me a hand occasionally. He noticed the difference between then and now. "It used to be fun," he said, "fighting and snapping heads. We were right upfront. None of this ambush stuff. What we've become are businessmen with guns."

Happy Jack was right: we had no heart. Each morning I showered and shaved, then walked to Mike's Barber Shop on the corner to have my hair blow-dried and hot-combed. I dressed like John Travolta and wanted to be James Dean.

It wasn't until March 1972 that the police and DEA started focusing on me. I'd avoided attention by tightening my circle to a few very trusted friends, a move dictated by common sense and what I saw happening around me. Dealers—criminals of any stripe, for that matter—usually get brought down by snitches, and these rats, more than anything else, began taking a heavy toll on drug pushers in my section of New Jersey. The truth is, Sherlock Holmes was a fictional character with few, if any, real-life counterparts. An actual detective is only as effective as his snitches.

A friend of a relative dimed me out. Busted with an ounce of pot, he bought freedom by telling what he knew about me. I learned what happened from my relative, vowed to kill the snitch but never got around to it, and ended up forgiving him.

It was a bad time, people dying left and right. My friend Happy Jack OD'd. Another biker brother, Rabbit, tried suicide by aiming a bullet at his heart, but managed mainly to damage his brain. Three other friends were killed in short order: Muskrat, an ex-Pagan and drug dealer, engineered a sensational escape from custody only to be gunned down by rival pushers as he sat in his car; the cops killed Tommy Haynes after a holdup; and they blew Tommy Astorina away during a gun battle. The police weren't playing games.

Recently I made a list of the thirteen people I considered my best friends during the 1960s–1970s. Only three of them are still alive.

A few days after learning about the snitch, I found out that police had been spotted taking pictures of my house from an unmarked car parked down the street. Reverting to my biker days, I rounded up some ex-outlaws and made plans to deal with this new threat. Our hijinks had worked in the past, hadn't they? I'd never gone to jail as a biker leader, had I? Why not employ tactics from the past? At least that was my reasoning, if such it could be called.

When the cops appeared the next afternoon, we were ready for them. I'd been waiting in the Porky Pig van, and started my own camera rolling. Then I whistled to my friends, who raced from the house and joined me adjacent to the window of the unmarked car from which a cop was shooting pictures. Our choreography was perfect. The six of us turned our backs to the camera, dropped our pants, and mooned the camera and the officers, their mouths agape with shock and surprise.

The shock and surprise quickly turned to anger. The leader of their two-man crew, a detective named Argentiare, cranked his engine, threw it in reverse, and peeled rubber back down the street. Argentiare got even more steamed after he circled the block and, with his partner shooting pictures out the window, was greeted again by six moons hangin' in the breeze.

Argentiare couldn't have been any hotter than I was. I built myself into a righteous rage about his invading my privacy and decided to give him a taste of his own medicine. I learned where this Rahway cop lived and, armed with a small camera and flash cube, headed for his house.

It was warm that night and his front door stood open. I peered through the screen and saw him sitting on a sofa, wearing Bermuda shorts and a T-shirt, watching television. It was good for him that I hadn't come as a cop killer because he'd have been a dead man— he never noticed me standing there.

I started snapping pictures through the screen, the flash cube popping, and Argentiare cursed and dove for cover. I knew I'd caught him in mid-leap, laughed, and stepped down off the porch. He came running, gun in hand, to the door.

"Are you crazy, punk?" he said, when he saw who I was. He had the gun aimed at my chest.

"Hey, Argentiare," I said, betting my life he wouldn't shoot, "you want a photo contest, I'm game." I couldn't resist. "I'll bet I look a million times better than that shot of you scrambling in fear."

"I want that film."

"No way, cop."

He could try to take it, but I didn't like his chances. He could shoot me and take it, but who knew how that scene would finally play?

Argentiare came through the screen and *asked* me to sit on the steps with him.

"I don't sit with cops," I said. Argentiare was every inch a cop. He'd first try to scare me, and if that worked, he'd offer a deal. It wouldn't work. There wasn't an ounce of rat in me.

But he tried. "Look, punk," he growled, "I know about the dope you keep down in your cellar. I know the names of your suppliers. I even know the location of that secret compartment in your van. I can take myself right to it. You need to talk to me while I'm still willing to listen."

That's the last thing I needed, told him so, and left. A cardinal rule: A criminal should *never* talk to the cops. The cop is not his friend, no matter what he says; in fact, he hates criminals. The overwhelming majority of prisoners blab their way into a cell. They rat themselves out.

Nonetheless, what Argentiare said alarmed me. At the least, I needed to make some changes, tighten up my act, move a bunch of things around. Perhaps the answer was running. I hadn't run after Tony Santa snitched and paid a heavy price. Only fools fail to learn from their mistakes.

Still. If Argentiare really had me by the nuts, like he said, why did he dillydally around taking pictures of my house? Why didn't he just bust me and then try the "I'm your friend" routine?

I needed time to sort things out, to chart the most prudent course of action, and then to act quickly. I thought of places to hole up and think the predicament through. However, before reaching a decision, a phone call came from a very unusual source—a cop—that resulted in a meeting which I can only describe as bizarre. I can't name the cop (referred to here as Hodge) because he's still in law enforcement.

"Minucci?"

"Yeah."

"This is Hodge. You know me."

"Yeah."

"Haul yourself over to Larry's. I want to see you."

Larry's was a Rahway bar. The way Hodge sounded, he'd imbibed a few too many.

"Argentiare tell you to call me?"

"I'm calling on my own."

"I don't talk to cops."

"Minucci, I genuinely hate you. You know that, don't you?"

"Yeah." I did know it. Hodge was an absolute straight arrow who viewed, with justification, people like me as scum. The thing about him, the reason I stayed on the line, he didn't have a devious bone in his body. I couldn't imagine his offering a deal. Maximum Hodge. His idea of justice was a clanging cell door and a permanently lost key.

"Well, I'm here at Larry's," Hodge slurred. "Come if you want to. I'll say this, you're the biggest fool in the world if you don't hear me out."

What harm could it cause? Just in case, though, I stuck a .357

snub in my belt before driving the GTO to Larry's. I found the husky Hodge hunched over a drink at a back table. There were three other customers, all at the bar, a vacant pool table, and a country singer wailing on the jukebox. I paid for a beer at the bar and carried it to the table.

"You don't look so good," I said. Actually, I thought a few more drinks would put him out. His eyes were red, puffy, and his hair disheveled. I sat down and had the distinct feeling he'd prefer not to be in the same country with me, much less sharing a small table in an intimate, dimly lit neighborhood tavern. "What's this important message you got?" I said.

"Get one thing clear in your mind," he said, his eyes glued to his drink. "I'm not doing this for you."

"Doing what?"

"Telling you to get out of town. Leave the state. Go to Mexico or Canada. Just get out."

"*Why* are you telling me this?"

"Be grateful I am. Or don't be grateful. Take off. Take off now."

"How do I know this isn't something you cooked up with Argentiare?"

But looking at him, three sheets to the wind, I found it difficult to picture Hodge as part of some intricate conspiracy. "Why are you telling me this?" I asked again.

"Just do what I say."

"Why?"

"Today's Friday, right?" He didn't seem sure. "Monday, bright and early, a world of cops, led by Argentiare and DeStefano, is going to hit you like a sack of cement. DeStefano, more than Argentiare, wants you rotting in jail forever. You'd better be gone before it happens."

"Why are you telling me this?" I asked a third time.

I don't think a sober Hodge would have confided in me. But he had come this far, and figured I wouldn't do as he said without knowing. "The force," he said, and I could tell that talking to me was almost killing him, "did me a rotten turn. I won't say what it was, but I deserve a lot better. Now, they want you bad. They've invested a lot of time and money in this bust. It's all set for Monday, like I said. So you want to know why I'm warning you. This is why: Because it's my way, just a little way, of getting back at them."

My mind raced, screaming at me that Hodge told the absolute truth. Even Argentiare's letting me walk away from his home served as confirmation. Argentiare knew my time was coming. I looked at Hodge, staring into his empty shot glass. He didn't want to hear thanks from me so I repaid the favor by leaving.

By the next morning, Saturday, I knew what I had to do. I rented a pair of U-Haul trailers and spent the afternoon loading up our furniture and clothes. "Where are we going?" Mary asked. "Florida," I said.

"Not me," she said. "The time to head to Florida is winter. Summer's coming on. We'll drown in our own sweat. I hear Florida is infested with mammoth flying cockroaches, bloodsucking mosquitos, and—"

"Shut up. Help me pack." If it had been only the two of us, I'd have left her behind. But we were six, not two, and I knew she wouldn't take care of the kids.

I had a few thousand dollars but, more importantly, 500 pounds of grass. We'd never go hungry with a stash that large. We could live a long time on a quarter-ton of marijuana—it's easier to sell than gold and appeals to a wider clientele: rich and poor, yuppies, grannies, workers, bosses, even cops. The marijuana was my security blanket. We didn't stand a chance in a new environment without resources. After a while, I figured, when the heat cooled down, I'd find a steadier line of work.

Still, a "few thousand dollars" ($4,281, to be exact—I counted it) wasn't enough to get settled in a strange place—not with a wife and four children—so after berating myself for an orgy of profligate spending and handouts to friends, I looked to add to my cash supply.

I knew just the person: Dudie Boyer, a drug dealer who lived in a big house a few towns away. Dudie was perfect. This short, thin, flashy-dressing dope peddler viewed me as a competitor and several times tried to shut me down—on the last occasion, for good. He'd paid a couple wannabes to drive by Mike's Barber Shop and whack me when I walked out. But they were nervous and couldn't shoot straight from a moving car, though they did blow out Mike's windows.

I hadn't gotten around to retaliating yet. Now I would. The plan was to grab Dudie, hold him hostage, scare him real good, and offer him his life in exchange for his money. Once I had the money I might or might not kill him: it depended on his attitude after I took his cash.

I called my friend Richie, 300 pounds of pro wrestler, a gentle, even-tempered guy always cast as the "heavy" in his matches. Placid and by nature nonviolent, he looked the part of evil incarnate—tattoos everywhere, small, beady eyes, shaved head, hard beer gut, massive torso, bulging arms, thick, powerful legs—and best of all, he could act. Wrestling crowds loved to hate him. His face bore a hundred scars. "The blood in the ring is real," he told me. "We cut our faces with razor blades. The more we bleed, the more we get paid."

We arrived at Dudie's darkened house at 1 A.M. Sunday morning. Figuring he was asleep, I popped the front door lock with a credit card and we went inside to look around. Nobody was home.

We searched the place, taking our time, using flashlights and keeping our ears cocked. I wanted Dudie to show up. Whatever we found lying around would compare as nothing to what we could get when he realized his life depended on raising a bundle.

I had no doubt Dudie would pay handsomely. At this time there had been a series of kidnappings of Mafiosi in New York (pulled off by a wild young gang of independents), and the Mob always paid. What good is money if you're dead? The positive part of such kidnappings: the police never got called. The negative part, which far outweighed the positive: the wiseguys would hunt you forever, and when they found you, you'd wish they had called the cops.

This score was different. Dudie wasn't connected, and even if he recognized me, I didn't fear the kind of people he could muster to retaliate. He didn't know Richie, had never laid eyes on him, and despite my friend's distinctive physical appearance, Dudie would realize he couldn't strike back without proof positive. Richie had pals in high places.

Richie found money—about $10,000 in cash—in a bottom

dresser drawer in the master bedroom, and I located a sturdy, bolted-down safe in the basement. I imagined it contained dope, maybe jewelry and more cash, but we hadn't come equipped to break, pry, or blow it open.

As we prepared to leave, about 2:30 A.M., we heard a car pull into the driveway, and a single door open and close. When Richie grabbed and I stuffed a sock into the mouth of the silhouetted figure reaching for the light switch, we both knew we had the wrong person. Dudie's wife.

Terror danced in her eyes. I spoke softly, calmly: "We won't hurt you if you answer a few questions."

She tried to struggle, but Richie held her as easily as he might a child.

"Listen to me," I said. "You won't be hurt if you cooperate. Do you understand?"

Having no choice, she managed a tight nod, her features contorted by panic. I waited several moments before removing the sock.

"Where's your husband?"

"He's . . . he's away."

"Where?"

"New York."

"When will he be back?"

"A . . . a few days."

"I guess we'll just have to wait for him," I bluffed.

"Please . . ."

"You won't be harmed. Unless it turns out you lied. He comes home early and you're dead."

We forced her at gun point to open the safe. Inside we found another $18,000 in cash, a .38 snub nose, and a bunch of personal papers. We marched her back upstairs.

I stuffed the sock back in her mouth and Richie carried her to a sofa. "See what kind of provisions they got," I told Richie, and settled in an easy chair opposite the sofa, as if preparing for a long wait.

It took fifteen minutes to convince me she had told the truth. Frightened as she was, she gave no clue that she expected Dudie's early arrival. Of course, hanging around a "few days" made no sense. I found a couple of belts in a downstairs closet and secured her in a manner I felt would hold for an hour or so.

Richie and I split, dividing the money as he drove. He dropped me off at the Pontiac I'd parked in a shopping mall and I said goodbye.

"Where you headed, brother?" he asked.

"Florida. Better if you don't know more than that."

"Keep in touch."

"You can count on it."

I'd been moving breakneck style since the warning from Hodge, but several more bases remained to be touched. There were people who counted on me that I wanted to let know I was heading underground. Fortunately, these were night people, so 4 A.M. to 6 A.M. was the ideal time to find them. My first stop: a poker game in Elizabeth.

Everybody had friends in Florida. "You need anything, just call my pal. Here. Let me write down the number. Tell him I sent you."

And deals. At least two dozen I could easily step into. In reality, some of them might not have been bad. And the guys endorsing me, at least a few, while viewed as "undesirable" by straight society, had strong credentials in my world.

I must have gathered a dozen names and phone numbers. Acting grateful—I really was—I nonetheless knew what I required was a low profile. Some of the "positions" I heard about would draw cops like flies to a picnic.

My last stop—at 6 A.M.—was at Blackie Zeal's house. Two hours too early for Blackie and Barbara, but they were glad I'd come by. I told them about Hodge and the need to leave Jersey, and Blackie judged I was doing "the right thing. Stay off the junk and maybe you got a fighting chance."

"Thanks to you, I've learned that lesson," I said resolutely, never dreaming that Demon Dope lay in wait to ambush me down the road.

"Buddy, one day at a time."

"I'll think about your backyard if I'm tempted," I said, and we all laughed, hugged, and said so long. I patted the big brown dog before driving off.

When I reached home, the kids were ready, but Mary was not. She still wanted to argue about Florida, and when I wouldn't budge on that, she launched into an intentionally irritating stall. Should I take this hair dryer? Or that one? "A girl needs to be sure." How many pairs of shoes? Shoes for eating out, or shoes for Okefenokee? What about makeup? Could we stop at a drugstore and stock up? "Come on," I said, "you're not gonna need all that." When she continued to stall, I grabbed her by her hair.

I led her outside, shoved her into the driver's seat of the GTO parked behind the van, and said, "Don't lose sight of Porky Pig."

Chapter 6

Not until we crossed into Connecticut did Mary realize something was wrong. She began honking the GTO's horn, and a glance at the side rearview mirror revealed her gesturing frantically, urging me to pull off on the shoulder and stop.

I smiled and kept going. There would be a Roy Rogers not far ahead. She could wait till then, until we were quietly seated in a booth.

Ronald, Jay, and Candice rode with me, playing in the back of the van, while our youngest, Keith, sat strapped in a safety seat next to his mom. Each of us pulled a U-Haul trailer packed with belongings.

Why was I going north? she'd want to know, when our destination was south. *Because you no doubt would have told your boyfriend, and he might have toughed out a full ten seconds of mild interrogation before coughing up the information.*

To be fair I could have said, but didn't, that I'd misled my own friends. Likely there was an informant or two, whose identity would surprise me, or a guy willing to trade for a better deal by chirping, "Minucci? Oh, yeah. He's down there with the gators."

In fact, something of this sort happened. I later learned the cops concentrated their search on Florida. The news pleased me, and so did finding out that Argentiare and DeStefano had argued with each other about blame after their Monday morning raid on an empty house.

Just to be difficult, I still wouldn't tell her where we were headed as we munched burgers and fries at Roy Rogers. "You'll love it," I said, though I didn't believe either of us would. *It's better than prison,* is what I thought.

We drove through Connecticut, part of Massachusetts, touched a tip of New Hampshire, and finally arrived in Maine. Already we were well above Canada's southernmost border and still had a good distance to go. Maine, which I envisioned as tiny, is four times larger than Massachusetts, but has fewer people.

I needed to pay close attention to directions. The Bangor realtor I'd called the morning before had listened to my fairy tale about burnout in the big city, an aggressive, heartless boss, the rat race of getting and spending in the "urban jungle" (he said he understood my "alienation"), and told me, not surprisingly, "I have just the place."

I didn't believe him. "Look, pal," I almost told him, "I don't want *any* nosy people around. Are you sure you understand that?"

Instead I said, "I'm talking about *really* isolated. Clear my head by returnin' to nature."

"I heard you, son."

He gave me directions which I copied carefully, telling myself not to be fooled by his honest-sounding Yankee accent. I said I'd arrive late Sunday night or early Monday and asked where I could pick up the key.

"It's under the mat."

"You're gonna leave it under the mat?"

"That's where it's been for six months."

"I'll stop by Monday with the rent and a deposit."

"No hurry, son. Get yourself settled first."

Now I drove through Bangor, Eddington, Veazie, the university town of Orono. After Stillwater I came to Old Town, a tiny hamlet famous for manufacturing quality canoes, and then, sticking to Highway 2A along the Penobscot River, I slowed to a crawl to look at signs. At last I found it, the misnamed French Settlement Road—more of a trail than a road.

French Settlement Road ran three miles to dead end at a junkyard. I know because I missed my driveway and traveled its entire length. Finally I turned the Porky Pig van around in a space that would have challenged a VW bug, and listened to Mary complain.

I found the driveway on the trip back. Actually, it was a narrow, 150-foot dirt path that bumped up a hill to a cleared-out plateau where sat our mobile home. I couldn't tell much about the place in the dark, and electric power had long since been cut off. The key, as promised, was under a large WELCOME TO OUR HOME mat, the exact opposite message I intended to convey. I unlocked the door, gathered blankets from one of the U-Hauls, and told everyone we'd camp on the living room floor. The kids were enthusiastic. Mary sulked, but could tell the time was wrong to give me lip.

My oldest, Ronald, woke me at 10 A.M., tugging on my arm. "Daddy! Daddy!" he said. "Come outside and see the big dog!"

Blinking sleep out of my eyes, I went out the front door, around the mobile home, and gasped in surprise when I saw our backyard: about twenty yards of grass and weeds ending abruptly at a tightly packed, impenetrable wall of tall trees.

"See the dog, Daddy!" Ronald cried, pointing to the edge of woods on my left.

There were three of them, a mother and two young ones. Because of his height and the brushy overgrowth that reached above my knees, Ronald had seen only the adult: a mother black bear out foraging with her cubs. Being a brick and pavement guy, I scooped up my son, scrambled around the mobile home to the front door, and locked it when I got inside.

Everyone except Mary wanted to go back out and see what I assured them were bears. I told them the animals were dangerous and they'd *never* be allowed outside to play if they didn't promise to steer clear of them. I didn't say it, but I figured we wouldn't be here long if the bears were regular visitors.

I explored the mobile home and liked what I saw: two big bedrooms, a large living room, a kitchen, two bathrooms, and a laundry room. The furniture we'd brought, and some I needed to buy, would make the place more than livable.

An hour later I cautiously ventured outside and determined the bears had moved on. Everyone piled out of the mobile home and got a first daylight glimpse of the neighborhood. The frontyard, like the back, was maybe twenty yards of clearing, badly overgrown now but I could fix that. The frontyard ended where the trees had not been cut down.

The large four-year-old mobile home looked good from the outside, too—a steal at $250 a month. It featured a decklike porch with wicker chairs and a swinging couch (the only furniture left behind). The kids retrieved a couple balls from a U-Haul and tossed them around.

I couldn't see French Settlement Road from the property, but that didn't mean we wouldn't be glimpsed from there. I trudged down the bumpy dirt path I called a driveway to get a look from below. The mobile home, if someone were really looking, was barely visible through a wall of tall birch, pine, and poplar trees. For reasons of security—false peace of mind, really—I preferred total invisibility.

Our first day was spent moving belongings from the two U-Hauls into the mobile home. At least we had beds to sleep on that night. The next morning we dropped the U-Hauls in Bangor (I'd rented them using fake ID), then spent the day paying the rent and deposit, and arranging the hookup for electricity needed for lights, heat, and power to pump water from the well. Unlike its counterparts in New York or New Jersey, the local utility didn't require a life history, personal and financial references, or a huge deposit. Twenty-five dollars took care of it all.

I spent a week learning my surroundings. Only three other families, all related, lived on French Settlement Road, the nearest a mile away. The men were lumberjacks and, I judged, live-and-let-live sorts who wouldn't stop by to engage in idle chitchat.

As my exploration expanded, I came across a hippie commune located a few miles up a little-traveled county road. Knowing the time might come when I'd need to sell some of my 500 pounds of grass—I stopped and introduced myself. The leader—everyone called him "Father"—wore bib overalls and a straw hat, reminded me of Rip Van Winkle, despite being only thirty-eight, and impressed me as well educated and well organized. The entire commune, in fact, about seventy-five people, had its act together. They'd built small homes and established their own school.

"We're entirely self-sufficient," Father said proudly, showing me several abundantly stocked root cellars and the cabin where they made crafts (macramé belts, wall hangings, pot slings, tie-dyed T-shirts, love beads, etc.) to sell to the public. Quality stuff. I bought T-shirts for the kids and a wall hanging for our living room.

"The cops don't hassle you?" I asked.

"We've never seen a lawman out here," Father answered. "There's no need for them, I guess."

And I didn't see any either—not one—until the very tag end of my two-year stay in Maine.

Still, I had an urban siege mentality. I learned residents could buy virtually any gun they wanted, and I accumulated an arsenal of pistols, rifles, and shotguns, enough to pin down a small army. My favorite was a 444 Merlin mag lever action, with scope, that could drop a full-grown moose at 100 yards with a single shot.

I surprised myself by adapting happily to rural life. I cleared the front, back, and side lawns, planted vegetable and flower gardens, and built a log fence around the mobile home from white birch. We could have done without electricity, as the hippies did, but everyone wanted TV. Our set pulled in about six channels, all of them fuzzy, and as time went by, we watched them less and less.

We camped and fished and hunted: rabbit, quail, ducks, Canadian geese. Deer, moose, and bear foraged near the mobile home. They honored our space and we conceded theirs.

Spring, when we arrived, was glorious, usually bright blue skies and air so fresh we could taste it; summer days were 80 degrees, 55 at night, great for sleeping; autumn was my favorite, crisp and bracing, whole forests changing colors, heaven painted red, brown, and bright orange; and winter, deep piles of snow, dazzling, sparkling white, stinging our eyes in the cold brilliant sunshine, not sooty and speckled a dirty black, as in New Jersey, plus temperatures often far below zero—but a dry cold that made it bearable.

Physically, I became a specimen. Hard all over. The manual

labor did it, and early to bed, early to rise. I muscled up to more than 200 pounds.

The nearest school was seventeen miles away, but Maine had a system whereby the teacher came to you. They were called traveling tutors, and they drove from home to isolated home giving personalized instruction. Two of our children were school-age, and I think they learned more in a familiar environment than they might have in a conventional classroom. They did lots of home study, assigned by the tutor, to make up for the necessarily shorter hours. In the dead of winter, of course, when roads were impassable, they had to do all the work assignments with help only from their parents.

Even Mary, the former party girl, accustomed herself to the new surroundings and began settling in. She had especially liked the fast, forget-about-the-future style I'd embraced, but now, if not content, at least seemed less wild and restless.

"You're getting with the program," I told her one afternoon as she packed clothes into the washer.

"Yeah?"

"Why do you think that is?" She had never shown the slightest inclination toward domesticity.

"Maybe because, for the first time, you're home."

Right, but I was home *too much*, I began to believe. A negative side to the isolation involved all the time it gave me to worry about my fugitive status. I couldn't forget that a long hard prison sentence awaited if some cop nailed me, and I regarded such an outcome as unacceptable. I invested many weeks familiarizing myself with the woods around me, and back roads I might use if I suddenly had to flee.

But wasn't jail precisely what I'd face when some neighbor—probably the wife of one of those lumberjacks—got suspicious of the family with no visible means of support? Or perhaps that realtor would nose around to check on how we were doing.

With hindsight, I realize it wouldn't have happened. Those independent wilderness people had a bone-deep respect for privacy, probably a mistrust of police also, and I never saw the realtor again. He didn't even show up to raise the rent. I mailed him a money order the first of each month and that was it.

Such was my paranoia, though, that I decided to become *more* visible. In April, about a year after arriving in Maine, I took a job driving a tractor-trailer for Diamond International, a paper company. I transported logs and pulp chips from lumber camps to a processing plant in Brewer, just south of Bangor.

The job brought me in contact with other workers; soon I was accepting invitations to have a few beers at quitting time. I liked the rough blue-collar atmosphere and humor, learned about ice hockey—Maine's state sport—plus, most significantly, discovered that while there were plenty of bars and booze, a marked shortage existed for another product these guys wanted: marijuana. I hinted I might have a solution.

Except for a few pounds I'd sold to the chronically short-of-cash hippie commune, I still had all the grass I'd brought north with me. Using that, I was once again in the drug business, and without the cutthroat competition existing in New Jersey.

Why did I do it? I could have lived comfortably forever on that little protected hill off French Settlement Road. Again, I think, it was fear of not having enough *things*. Within a month, I'd bought two canoes, two snowmobiles, and a brand new runabout boat.

Word spread, and I knew the time would come when I'd need a fresh supply of weed. The demand was enormous, and not just from teenagers and workers. People you wouldn't think would touch the stuff enjoyed their marijuana, for entertainment and relaxation. Rich and poor of all ages loved the mellow high that grass gave them. Quicker than liquor and no hangover.

One of my customers, a junkyard owner named Ed, confided that "we" could "make some real money" if I had "good" connections back home.

"What you got in mind, Ed?" I asked.

"Can I trust you?"

What a question to ask me.

"You can trust me, Ed."

"It's a little complex. Devious, you know."

"Try me."

Ed rambled, related things out of order, simplifying the complicated, and vice versa, but what it reduced to was a very sweet stolen car racket. The scheme relied on the lack of a Maine law, a carryover from more honest times, requiring titles for automobiles. In fact, the people of Maine didn't use titles. The only red tape for selling a car was your word on a sheet of paper saying you'd sold it—Vehicle Identification Number (VIN) such-and-such—to Mr. Whomever for a given amount of money. You then took the sheet of paper to the Motor Vehicle Department, whose representative in our area was a nearly blind, nice old lady in her eighties who'd been representing the state out of her home since the days of Henry Ford. She'd chat for a while, then stamp the sale official and send the paperwork to the capital, Augusta.

The key was obtaining actual VINs, strips of metal with the numbers on them, riveted to various spots on the car: the engine compartment, chassis, dash, and inside the driver's door. This is where Ed came in. He dealt in wrecked cars, buying them for salvage, and it was a piece of cake for him to pry off the VINs and attach them to a different automobile. Say someone totaled a new Cadillac. If he could find a Caddy of identical model and year, he'd switch the VINs and sell it at irresistible discounts. That's where I came in.

"How many wrecks a month do you handle?" I asked.

"I average about four. I only want fairly new merchandise." Ed said he had a deputy sheriff brother-in-law who tipped him to "all the good crashes." He often arrived at wreck scenes with a tow truck before the victims were moved.

"Does your brother-in-law know about this plan?" I asked.

"Not a chance. No way. He thinks he's doing a favor for the family."

Four cars a month wasn't enough, I decided. I told Ed he needed to expand, shoot for becoming the Junkyard King of Maine, but certainly a wider area than he currently covered. His brother-in-law would admire his ambition and pass the word to neighboring law enforcement buddies that Ed treated people right.

"You mean slip a cop some money?" Ed asked. "Like give him fifty dollars?"

"That what you pay your brother-in-law?"

"Yeah," he said, looking sheepish.

I thought, *So much for "doing a favor for the family."* Out loud I said, "Fifty bucks sounds about right."

"You sure you got the connections to handle all these cars."

"I got the connections," I said. I planned on calling Richie and Blackie Zeal.

More than a year had passed since I'd talked to either of them, but they had the sense not to ask questions. I said I'd meet them the next evening, 7:30, in the lounge at Newark's Holiday Inn.

I could feel the adrenaline pumping on the Bangor-to-Newark flight. It was always this way, before a bike run, a stickup, or kicking somebody's ass. It's called a rush. Athletes experience rushes, and they're positive things, when controlled, sharpening the mind and body. Some guys break the law for the rush it provides. I envisioned the car scam operating on a much bigger scale than Ed did, and was eager to begin.

After a crunching bear hug from Richie, a handshake and "How ya doin'?" from Blackie, we sat at a table with a view of the pool and ordered drinks.

"You ain't gettin' much sunshine down south," Blackie said. I got the feeling he'd known, not my exact location, but that the Florida talk had been bull.

"How'm I standing here?" I asked.

"What do you think? You aren't Dillinger. The manhunt lasted about two weeks. Cops talked to everybody you know. Learned about Florida, I couldn't find out from who." He swallowed his drink and signaled for another. "I guess that's one rat you ain't worried about."

"Only one?"

"That's what I heard. Florida was alerted, but you know how that goes. They pick you up for jaywalkin' or speedin', they know to hold you. Life goes on. I hear Argentiare and DeStefano are very serious about this, but what can they do?"

"Hope I get busted, wherever I am."

"Right. To your credit, they're betting it will happen in Florida."

Richie spoke for the first time. "I gotta admit, I didn't think you'd look so good. You've been workin' out."

"And the 'cure's' still holding," Blackie added.

They didn't ask where I'd been. I didn't tell. We talked about mutual acquaintances and I learned that three more guys I'd been close with had been killed.

Finally we got down to business. I said I needed cars, not just any car, but ones I'd specifically order: a 1973 Lincoln, for example, with a bonus paid for the right color. I'd pick them up at Newark International.

"How many you gonna want?" Richie asked.

"At least one a week from each of you. This works like I think it will, I'll need more."

"One a week's not many," Blackie said. "Sounds nickel-and-dime to me."

I'm not exaggerating when I say a good car thief can grab ten vehicles a day. Hustle one to a chop shop (it's all parts thirty minutes later) and hurry out to get another. Unfortunately a kid, at $50 per, can clear $500 a day, a few thousand a week with Saturdays and Sundays off: A temptation too great for mechanically minded teenagers who otherwise would be pumping gas or flipping hamburgers for minimum wage.

Terrific earnings also for Blackie and Richie, I explained, a grand a week for a few hours' work. Fifty-two thousand a year, no strain, and that just for starters. "You'll only be snatching the best," I said.

"When do we start?" Richie asked.

"Right now, if you want," I said.

I'd come prepared. Ed had two luxury wrecks sitting in his junkyard, two Caddys, one new, the other a year old. "I'll take the new one," Richie said. "My neighbor, two doors down, just bought exactly what you need. When do you want delivery?"

"Tonight."

He rose to leave. "Bring it here," I said. "We'll do the airport routine next time."

Blackie and I settled back with another drink, recalling guys we knew and scores we'd pulled. It's what always happens when criminals get together: they talk about their lives, and that means crime. Blackie conceded that the stolen car racket sounded promising, but so had others that turned sour for us. "Barbara thinks we're cursed as a team," he said. "She loves you to death, but says we ought to be friends, not partners."

"Don't tell her."

"Yeah. But I wonder . . ."

Richie was back in two hours, a cat-that-swallowed-the-canary expression on his face. "It's parked in the rear," he said. "I gassed it up."

We had a last drink. Blackie asked when I wanted delivery from him, and I said I'd call in two days. I paid Richie, picked up my overnight bag, and headed out to find the Cadillac. I switched the New Jersey plate for the dealer plate I'd brought from Maine and drove—with one stop for gas—all the way to Ed's junkyard. I watched as he switched the VIN tags, then held out my hand.

"I ain't got that kind of money on me," he said.

"Then start carrying it," I said. "Payment is C-O-D. No credit. No delays."

And there weren't any from then on. I usually gave him my tough guy act (it wasn't always an act), and his fear discouraged any tendencies he might have had to play games. Also, he soon was making more money than he'd ever imagined. Despite his efforts, he couldn't manage more than two cars a week, but that came to $6,000 (before expenses) every seven days. A guy could fill shoe boxes fast at that rate.

Three days after my first flight to Newark, I made a second one to pick up the car Blackie stole. We worked everything out on the phone, even how he'd be paid, and we didn't have to see each other to make the exchange. Employing code during our conversations, we communicated without fear of others overhearing. Of course, we operated from pay booths just to be safe.

Twice-a-week was plenty for me. I've always been blessed with plenty of energy, but three New Jersey-to-Maine drives a week would have been too much. I could have hired a mule, I suppose, but what would have been in it for me? Sure, I could have paid a wage—say a thousand dollars a trip—and pocketed the difference, like godfathers do. But a trustworthy mule might have resented my greed, while a do-it-for-the-thrills type could get us caught. Such were my concerns in the parasitic life I'd chosen.

I stopped pressuring Ed to urge his brother-in-law to contact cops in even more distant locales. We had reached far enough, I decided. Besides, my marijuana business was booming, and supply was no longer a problem. When I ran short, I picked up what I needed in Jersey and transported it north in a stolen car.

My long, increased absences from our wilderness home resurrected the "Old Mary," always griping and sulking but never saying why. I tried placating her with wads of cash and household luxuries, but our relationship went from bad to worse.

Things between us became uglier even than before. In the past, at least, she had shared in some biker adventures, had friends she'd grown up with. Out in "nowhereland," as she called it, she'd grown sick of the scenery. For my part, I stayed away for longer periods of time. I had quit the job with Diamond International, but enjoyed drinking with my old trucker buddies.

I always bought rounds for everyone. Money had long ceased to be a concern. Six months in the marijuana and stolen car businesses had packed three shoe boxes full of cash. I kept the boxes hidden behind a heavy maple dresser in the main bedroom.

The winter of 1973–74 skidded the stolen car caper to a halt. I judged it suicide to drive stolen automobiles over some of those frozen roads. Much of the time I couldn't get out of my own driveway. My own moral bankruptcy kept me from fully appreciating the glorious winter that encased us.

I stopped by Ed's junkyard whenever I could, which wasn't often. His end of the business flourished. Icy roads meant lots of wrecks, and spring would mean three, even four, flights a week to New Jersey. *You can do it,* I told myself.

In mid-March 1974, I was itching to go. I called Richie and Blackie, told them what I needed, and booked a flight to Newark. I'd deliver a car to Ed, have him transport me to the Bangor Airport, and catch a few Z's on the plane. If anyone thought my frequent flyer show was suspicious, he or she never uttered a peep.

In late-May, just when I was catching up, looking forward to two-a-week, one disaster led to a second and did us in. First, Ed got sloppy with the VIN tags on a car he sold to a mailman: he forgot to switch the tag on the driver side door. The postman, so proud of his new automobile that he drove it on his rounds, had a fender-bender he called the sheriff's department to investigate.

Of course, they noticed the missing VIN, asked where he had purchased the machine, and visited Ed's junkyard.

Ed was out towing a car, so the law questioned a retarded youngster who worked for him. The kid said he didn't know about the missing VIN, but that Ed had gotten the car from me. I learned what happened when I arrived at the junkyard a few hours later.

Ed teetered on the edge of a breakdown, visions of the Big House dancing in his head. "I never should have let you get me into this," he said.

The idea had been his, but arguing wouldn't help. "Look," I said, "probably we can ride this out. But you gotta pull yourself together. They'll yank the VIN records, put them together with the traffic accident report, and figure you bought the car legit. We'll say I did a lot of work and fixed it good as new. Somehow one of those VIN tags got torn off and we're sorry."

"What if they learn the car is stolen?"

"They won't."

I *hoped* they wouldn't. I knew Maine cops didn't have fancy computer hookups, and doubted they could match a stolen New Jersey car with the one the mailman drove. A bigger danger involved any probe into my past—specifically, a fingerprint check. *Every* state had that capability, and I'd be nailed by the fugitive warrant. The key was avoiding the kind of suspicion that led to mug shots and fingerprinting.

I wasn't getting through to Ed. "I don't know," he said. "Maybe if we cooperate and confess, they'll go easy on us."

I blinked, wondering if I'd heard right, and considered what I could do about this guy. What we needed were zipped lips, not "cooperating" and "confessing."

Ed wanted to be punished, I figured, so he needed to be shown the downside of that course of action. He needed to be guided in a different direction.

I put my arm around his shoulders. "How long have you been married, Ed?"

"Twelve years." His eyes teared.

"Three kids, right?"

"Yes." He covered his face with his hands.

"Ed, think about what you're saying. If not for your own good, but for your wife and three little ones. What will this do to them? Their husband and daddy a crook. Friends shunning your wife, playmates making fun of your kids. Do you want to do that to them, Ed?"

"No." He sat down on the ground, hands still cradling his face.

Just to be sure, I ladled it on a little more. "Ed, the cops won't make a deal with you. Not one they will keep, anyway. You involved *them* in a crime. They'll see that you get the max."

Actually, they would cover up, save their own hides, and that did mean cutting a deal. With a good lawyer, Ed might walk.

"You can step away from this, Ed, and avoid hurting a lot of people, including your brother-in-law. Just tell 'em you bought a wrecked car and I fixed it. It's simple."

And it might have been, except for that second disaster. A week earlier I'd brought him an expensive pickup truck to substitute for a wreck he'd towed, but the buyer suffered an unexpected financial reversal and couldn't come up with the cash. It made Ed nervous having the pickup in his junkyard with VIN tags from a vehicle all the king's horses and men couldn't have repaired that fast. He whined so much I agreed to sell the pickup from the mobile home.

Before leaving Ed, I made sure he'd composed himself enough so that *maybe* he could sell our story to the cops. I said they'd be visiting us soon and "we're all counting on you."

Nothing happened for three long days. Ed thought maybe the cops "just dropped the matter"; I assured him they'd be around and to keep a grip on himself. "You're gonna be okay," I said.

The fourth afternoon a guy showed up at the mobile home to look at the pickup. He liked it, especially the price, and left a hundred-dollar deposit "to hold it till morning." Everything seemed straightforward; too straightforward, my instincts told me. I phoned a guy I'll call Tom, a drinking pal from Diamond International, and asked him for a favor.

The buyer showed up about ten the next morning. He brought a friend and a certified bank check with him. Now I knew something was wrong.

"I told you I wanted cash," I stalled. "I don't know if that check is good or not."

"Sign it," he said, "so we've got a receipt, and I'll give you the cash."

"The truck belongs to a friend of mine. I'm selling it for him."

"Where is this friend?"

"Asleep inside. I'll have him endorse your check and be right out."

In the mobile home I called on my acting experience from Jamesburg reformatory, using a second voice for the guy I supposedly woke up. Mary looked at me oddly. The kids didn't have a clue. I signed the check with my left hand and carried it outside. They paid in hundred-dollar bills, sixty-nine of them, and left in two vehicles.

The call from Tom came a couple minutes later. "Two guys just leave your house?" he asked.

"Yeah."

"I just saw them at the entrance to French Settlement Road. Talking to the sheriff. He and some deputies have blocked your road."

I hung up, figuring I didn't have much time. It had been a good idea, having Tom keep watch, but he'd been three miles from the nearest phone. They might already be on their way back. Having carried the sting this far, they had surely found the wrecked pickup from which the VINs came, and they wouldn't fool around. With every nerve in my body screaming *run*, I risked a last phone call to Ed.

"You heard anything?" I asked.

"They're here now! At least a dozen feds!"

I dropped the receiver and raced outside. There wasn't a second to waste. "I'll send for you and the kids," I shouted to Mary and gunned the car down the driveway.

Chapter 7

I turned left out of the driveway and drove to the dead end. There, having two years ago anticipated the need for escape, I drove fifteen feet on a path I'd cleared to railroad tracks that sliced through the deep woods. I nearly tipped the car over getting the right side tires between the tracks; tires on the left side had to find precarious purchase on the narrow gravel embankment. Once straightened away, I steered a slow, bumpy ride over wood ties for two miles till I reached an old unused lumber road that intersected, in another mile, with a state highway. Maneuvering the right side tires over the track required going forward an inch, back an inch, forward again, infinite patience required from a guy in a hurry and on the run. Several times I thought the GTO would topple on its side.

I found the state highway and aimed the car north, away from where the pursuit originated, and soon found myself in wilderness. Nobody lived where I drove, or if they did, I didn't see them. It was just me, a road that got worse, and millions of trees. I finally stopped outside Caribou, near the border with New Brunswick, Canada, and rented a motel room.

That night I saw myself on TV: wanted for selling drugs and running a stolen car ring, which must have meant Ed—surely he'd talked—because no one knew about Blackie and Richie except me. The picture flashed on the screen was Frank Minucci, all right, but the picture was ten years old. "Armed and dangerous," said the perky lady newscaster, "and last seen driving a 1968 Pontiac GTO."

I took stock of my plight, deciding first I'd have to gamble that the motel guy didn't watch the TV news, and wouldn't put two-and-two together even if he did. So I would stay, at least for the night. Driving around in this no-man's-land seemed infinitely more dangerous than remaining put.

Cashwise I was okay for the short run. Thanks to those cops, I had $7,000, about what I'd come to Maine with, but I needed to be careful. Certainly the serial numbers had been copied. More important, I had a great deal more money back at the mobile home. With luck, the shoe boxes would be waiting when I sent someone for Mary and the children.

I believe, if a guy's not already brain-dead (too many criminals are), he thinks clearest when he's on the lam. He has to—it's that or his life.

What likely would get me caught? I wondered. Two things: my looks and that car. I'd take care of both the moment I could.

But not in Caribou. I didn't think anybody who looked like me had ever come to Caribou. I'd stick out like a smog cloud in this clear, clean place.

Early the next morning I headed for Augusta, Maine's capital, south and west of Bangor. They wouldn't figure I'd go there, I thought, but more important I wanted to lose myself among people.

Fifty miles out of Caribou I spotted a highway patrol car in the rearview mirror, a quarter-mile back but coming fast. I floored the GTO—it could never outrun the trooper—and the cop flipped on his lights and siren. I grabbed the only chance I had, turning onto another old logging road, and the chase was on. Police love chases; no matter what they say, they become kids playing real-life cops-and-robbers.

While the trooper with his souped-up cruiser had the advantage on open road, he needed to ease back on the logging trail or risk hurtling into tall trees. The road figured to peter out at an abandoned camp or, rather, to make a U-turn and come back in the opposite direction on a parallel path. When I'd put maybe a quarter-mile between me and the trooper, I gambled on a left turn, plowed through some heavy brush, and found the road going back. I waited till the cruiser bumped by going the opposite way, then had to cross a small wooden bridge before reaching the highway again. I stopped, doused some branches with some Coleman Lantern fuel I kept in the car, and set the bridge ablaze.

I finally made it to the outskirts of Augusta, a remarkable stroke of luck, since I later learned the law searched for me with helicopters and even a plane. In New York or New Jersey stolen cars would have been a low priority. In Maine they made a big noise.

I sold the GTO to a used car guy outside Augusta, walked a half-mile to a second buy-a-wreck joint, and paid cash for a beat-up green Chevy. After stops at a drugstore and thrift shop, I rented a motel room under the name of Andy Dale Corey, occupation traveling salesman (I liked that touch), and went to work on myself.

First came the self-administered haircut; it helped not caring how it came out. I intended to switch motels and pose as a lumberjack, a profession not noted for stylish coiffures. Aiming for the yokel look, I dyed blond what remained of my hair, shaved my mustache, and took out my false teeth (previous drug use had rotted out my bottom teeth and I wore a lower plate). The final touches were clear pink-framed glasses and a floppy hat purchased at the thrift store.

A week was all I could take of Augusta. There was nothing the town offered that held appeal for me, and besides I needed to gather up my family and those shoe boxes stuffed with money. I called Tom, the guy who'd served as lookout on French Settlement Road, and gave him the address of a dive halfway between Augusta and Bangor where we could meet the next afternoon.

I was the only patron in the bar when he arrived and still he didn't recognize me. "Pretty good, huh?" I said, shoving my mug up to his.

"Your own mother wouldn't know you."

"She wouldn't recognize me *without* the disguise," I said, "but that's another story. Look, I need your help. I want you to get my family and bring them here tomorrow."

"Won't the cops be watching?"

"My family? Not likely. At least not 'round-the-clock. I won't lie to you, Tom. It'll be risky, but you should come out good on this."

He waited.

"I got some expensive stuff at that mobile home. It's yours. All of it. And the van. You can have the van." I'd miss Porky Pig but he'd be like a neon sign pointing straight to me.

"Can I have the guns?"

"Everything but what Mary brings. Remind her to bring my shoes."

She'd know what that meant, I thought.

"What if they're watching?"

"Tell 'em you've come as a friend. If you're stopped on the way, say you're takin' her to family in New Jersey. You're a good samaritan. The dangerous part is when you get here. Be sure you're not followed."

"You can count on it. Word is they want you real bad."

"What else you hear?"

He averted his eyes.

"Tell me. I need to know."

"They're sayin' you're Mafia. That you're connected to a bunch of Italians in New Jersey."

A disaster, I thought. The Maine cops would love boasting how they saved their fair state by nipping an Italian invasion in the bud. The name "Minucci" was enough for them to think I was in the mob. In the long run, their thinking I was Mafia worked to my benefit, but who could have foreseen that?

Tom delivered my family promptly at 4 P.M. the next day. It made me want to pound myself seeing the worry and fear in my children's eyes; it was one thing to foul up my own life, another to hurt them. I wanted to say, "Daddy will make it all right for you," but the words would sound hollow, given my deeds, so I'd simply have to show them. Like a just-convicted man telling the judge, and meaning it at the moment, that he'd do better if given another chance, I vowed to turn my life around.

In the green Chevy, going south, Mary was part whimpering martyr, shrunken against the passenger door, and part avenging angel hissing answers to my questions through clenched teeth.

"Did you bring the shoe boxes?" I asked.

"They're gone. Like everything else, Frank, they're gone."

"What do you mean?"

"The police have them. At least I think they do. They ripped the place apart after you left."

"Did you look?"

"Of course I looked. Sure wished I'd thought to check it earlier. We'd have been long gone before Tom ever showed up."

The turn-my-life-around vow got put on hold less than half an hour after I'd made it. I'd already taken too many risks with that hot money. Like my looks and the GTO, I'd have to discard it. But for any new start I'd need a bankroll, need it fast, and the only ways I knew to get one were illegal.

I drove nonstop through the night to Linden, New Jersey, rented a cheap room—two lumpy beds with soiled sheets, dried vomit visible on the carpet, peeling paint, cockroaches—gave Mary money for food, and said I'd be back. I told the kids it would only be a day or so. It turned out to be ten.

I phoned Blackie and met him in a bar. "That's clever," he said, eying me head to foot.

"I need to score some money," I said. "You got any ideas?"

"Relax. You run out all tensed up in the middle of the day, the cops'll love it. Catch me up on your situation."

I did. For the first time he learned the details of the scam up in Maine. "I messed up again," I concluded.

"Don't talk that way. Don't get down on yourself. It was a sweet deal while it lasted. Nothin' goes on forever, not even pain." He eyed me again. "It's good to see you're still clean. Now, here's what I got . . ."

It seemed his nephew was dating a coin collector's daughter who had given the boy a peek at the treasure. What Blackie called a "discreet background check" (actually, all he did was ask his nephew) uncovered that the coin collector was an accountant, a small, mild-mannered nerd not likely to offer resistance.

Not that I would worry about resistance. I needed money right away and didn't care. A .38 makes everybody equal.

We came at 10 P.M. dressed in black and wearing ski masks. The door hadn't opened more than a half-inch in response to my knock when I shoved it open with my foot, grabbed the accountant, and jammed the barrel of the gun against the bridge of his nose. "Make one sound and I'll blow your head off."

The guy shook so bad I feared he'd suffer a coronary. Blackie stormed through the door behind me and headed for the sound of the TV in the den. He pointed his pistol first at the wife, then the daughter, and said calmly, "You can either live or die. It's up to you."

I pushed the accountant into the den and sat him on the sofa next to his family, then held the .38 on them while Blackie taped their hands, feet, and mouths. All except the accountant's mouth. We needed to hear him talk.

Blackie took a throw pillow and held it to the wife's head. In his other hand he pressed a gun to the pillow. I bent at the waist and planted my face an inch from the accountant's. "Listen carefully," I growled, "I'm gonna ask just once so pay attention. If you lie to me, my friend will put a bullet in your old lady's head. Now—where are the coins?"

"What coins?"

Blackie backhanded the guy's wife with the hand that held the pistol. I cracked the accountant on top of his head with the butt of mine.

"One last time. Where are the coins?"

"In the bathroom. Under the sink. Behind a panel. Take them but then, *please*, leave."

"Secured" in a portable safe deposit chest were scores of gold and silver coins—more than a hundred in all—each encased in plastic wrapping or little hard plastic boxes. Big coins and little coins, every one in "mint" condition. Like most guys in this kind of work, Blackie and I had no idea what they were worth. We'd have to rely on our fence, which is always a bad idea. We left the poor man and his family scared and shaking.

The fence said $15,000 top was what he'd pay. We took it. Later Blackie read in the paper that the accountant claimed a value of $200,000.

Three days went by before the coins were exchanged for spending money, a period of painful awareness of having broken my promise of just a "day or so" to my kids. That I stayed with them most of the time only made the place more packed and uncomfortable.

At last, money in hand, I drove to Staten Island, twenty minutes from Linden by bridge but a world apart, to find an apartment. I'd hid in the seclusion of Maine. One of the five boroughs of Manhattan, Staten Island in June 1974 featured a low-key, uncrowded rural ambience: small shops, pretty wooded parks, not a single tall building.

I was acquainted with Staten Island, knew it served as home to many wiseguys, and most importantly that law enforcement didn't overly concern itself with who lived there. The havoc mobsters might raise in other New York City areas was pretty much off-limits on Staten Island. Wiseguys kept their own nests clean, not just of their own activities but those of street hoods foolish enough to mistake tranquility for weakness.

It took just two days to find a comfortable basement apartment across from St. Rock's Church. I told the landlord that our apartment in Boston had burned—such a fire had recently made national news—and we'd decided to start over in New York, "a place I'd been stationed in the Navy," I lied. Most landlords would have demanded a life history, plus a battery of personal and employment references, but not this guy. "I make my own judgments," he said, "and I think you're okay. From what I hear, you've got a nice family. You've had some bad luck, so have I, but I know you're gonna pull through."

The fatherly man was determined to help. After I'd bought the necessary furnishings and moved the family from the motel, he stopped by and quickly befriended the children. "How are you managing?" he asked me.

"We'll be fine," I said.

He didn't believe it. "You okay on food?"

"We're fine."

"Found work yet?"

"I'm looking. Shouldn't be long."

The next day, no doubt at his prompting, parishioners from St. Rock's came bearing food and toys. The owner of a small grocery next to the church said he had started a tab for us. Our landlord himself stopped by that evening to ask if I'd like driving a bus to and from a private school. "Doesn't pay much," he said, "but it's a start."

I thanked him and took the job. I'd started looking for hustles, and a legit front could divert suspicion from other activities. In my shame and remorse at uprooting my children and turning them into fugitives, I'd considered becoming Joe Citizen, but what job skills did I have? Somehow brute force, drug dealing, and burglary just would not get me far in the straight world.

The best thing I could do for my children, I decided, was provide a comfortable life for them. I reasoned they'd be better off in Staten Island schools, and with my regular job, they wouldn't have to know how I kept us in steaks.

I thought about getting caught a few times, but a part of my mind always said, *Nah, it can't happen.* Having avoided capture for so long, I'd begun to believe that it wouldn't happen to me.

I met a few wiseguys through my Jersey connections, and others familiar with me because of my father's reputation. "What's the old man doing?" I'd be asked, and I could honestly answer, "I don't know." I wanted to add, "And I don't care."

I didn't expect immediate acceptance from the wiseguys. Some wannabes I encountered were full of themselves, talkin' the talk, gonna set the world on fire, always threatening to whack some guy. The people I needed to associate with were cautious and restrained, heavy on actions, light with words, and I knew they'd bide their time watching me. I hung around places where I'd be seen, not wearing a sign—POSITION WANTED—but available if needed.

Meantime, Blackie and I began hijacking trucks at Jersey rest stops, often two or three a week. We sold the loads—cigarettes, whisky, meat, expensive furs—to mob-connected middlemen. We even sold the stolen trucks for parts.

I renewed trusted biker connections, reestablished my source of marijuana supply, and started building a new clientele.

One thing I did that first autumn on Staten Island surprised everyone. I attended night school and earned a high school equivalency diploma. I figured *doing* it would be more effective than lectures to the kids about the need for education.

Previously we'd snatched bikes and other kids' stuff off suburban lawns, but on Christmas '74 we went all out. We grabbed a *trailer* full of toys—dolls, race car sets, electric trains, G.I. Joe trucks, and jeeps—in a freightyard near Newark. Not just our children, but those of friends, hit the jackpot that year. In fact, so did we. A wiseguy paid us $6,000 for the mountain of goods still left over.

I'd noticed in night school a potential for profit, so when a fellow student said I could go on to college and make money in the bargain, I listened. Since I'd been in the military, he reasoned, and hadn't been discharged dishonorably, I probably qualified for the G.I. Bill.

The government had never given me anything except pain, I thought, so why should it change now? But I checked it out and, incredibly, learned I could receive $412.64 every two weeks. I immediately registered at Staten Island Community College.

I learned a few things, especially in English and drama classes, which I thoroughly enjoyed. Of course, you couldn't avoid learning *something*, just sitting there, and I had strong motivation to attend: making money in an atmosphere craving for my services. As I'd suspected, college students, like everyone else, needed a reliable marijuana supply, and who better to provide it than me?

Getting good grades presented no problem. My underpaid teachers often needed loans, or wanted to put a bet down on a ballgame. Giving me a failing grade was unthinkable. First, most of them owed me—"You need nice wheels at a bargain price? Sure, I got just the thing"—and all were intimidated. I looked like the rough character I was, sounded the part, too. It would have taken a brave prof to flunk me.

I even worked on the college paper, *The Dolphin*, as a layout artist. A student wanting his article published had to deal with me, or somehow the story didn't appear. Often the price of publication was doing one of my homework assignments. Teachers practically begged me to turn in a paper or two, give them some justification for the passing grades, and wannabe *Dolphin* contributors obliged.

College didn't interfere with my other lucrative activities. These started to expand, as I'd suspected they would, when a few wiseguys cut me on some action. One of them, Big Sal, a major marijuana and THC dealer, wanted to move his wares into Staten Island's black community and I accepted the challenge.

I reached into the black neighborhood through a brother named Tasheem. Extremely antiwhite, versed in black and Islamic studies, he wore African garb and always had six guys around him. A "white devil" I might be, but soon he cut out the rhetoric to reveal his favorite color was green. I gave him a half-pound of pot on consignment, to see how he'd do, and an hour later he wanted more.

Tasheem was a natural. Soon, with pushers in every hangout and park, he was moving fifteen pounds of grass a week, and thousands of hits (at $3 per) of THC. Big Sal's affection for me grew each Friday night when I delivered a paper bag filled with money. I was an "earner," the highest praise the mob can offer.

Of course, there were problems. One of Tasheem's dealers, Junebug, consistently came up short on the count. When it reached $2,000, I went to see him, intending to send a message to all the pushers who dealt with us. I took Tasheem along, and a bone-breaker named Monty.

We found Junebug shooting hoops in a playground on Jersey Street. We got out of the car and Tasheem motioned him over.

"Brothers, what's happening?" Junebug greeted us.

Monty answered with a vicious short knockdown punch, then kicked him in the side. I cracked his skull with a ball-peen hammer. Neither the shrieks, mercy pleas, nor gushing blood elicited even a trace of compassion or softening of blows from me. This was taking care of business, an ugly but necessary part of the life I'd chosen. Tasheem turned away as the rise and fall of the hammer alternated with Monty's rib kicks.

We carried the twisted Junebug behind my new Thunderbird and tied his feet to the rear bumper. Off we drove through the project, his body bouncing, *scraping,* like a thrown rider dragged by a runaway horse, limp arms and bloody head bobbing, thumping helplessly, depositing a fluid and tissue crimson trail on the abrasive pavement. I stopped after two blocks, pleased to note that a crowd had gathered, straddled Junebug's mangled chest, shoved a .38 inside his mouth, and said, "Pay Tasheem every penny you skimmed from me by Friday, or we'll give you another ride. Only next time, I squeeze the trigger."

Junebug paid. And the bumper-bind-and-drag technique that produced fast results from slow payers became my trademark. Wiseguys, if asked to cite my most memorable quality, would probably recall how I collected debts.

I graduated from Staten Island Community College with a two-year associate degree. There was even a little ceremony. Mary didn't show up, but Blackie did. Many of my wiseguy friends poked fun at the accomplishment, but secretly I think they were envious. Some Mafiosi are genuine animals, proud of their ignorance, yet others are impressed by what they consider learning.

In October 1976, I was offered the manager's position at a Brighton Avenue after-hours club. It was a job indicating trust, and I took it. I wanted to get closer to the wiseguys. Often what they did involved big money; in comparison, my escapades with Blackie were penny ante. Also, never to be underestimated, the Mafia had friends in high places, plus access to bail money and skilled criminal attorneys. Any wretch languishing in the Tombs or Rikers Island, often on a petty charge, knows the importance of connections.

An after-hours club manager needs several strong job qualifications: He must be able to count and then justify the addition to the boss (mobsters, ever suspicious, *assume* they're being shorted); he needs to eliminate employee theft; he has to be a real hard nose at times, a tough bouncer, yet a diplomat when the situation demands; and he must know which customers receive markers (credit) and which ones don't.

The Brighton Avenue club featured strong drinks, music and a dance floor, two dice tables, plus poker and blackjack. Many customers, escorted by bartenders whose joints had closed, came for the hookers. The gambling, operated on a strictly "honest" basis, provided the lion's share of the profit. Over the long run, and usually the short, the house simply couldn't lose.

The clientele varied, some bigshots, some just average guys, but the "boys" were always around. A few times a guy burst in boasting who he was, who he was with, and a few days later I'd read about him in the paper: WISEGUY FOUND DEAD IN TRUNK OF PARKED CAR.

The loudmouths, as I've indicated, weren't the ones to watch. The up-and-comers, or those already arrived, never said much. They gambled and drank, had a good time, left big tips, and quietly faded out the door.

Just being in that environment brought numerous moneymaking proposals. One I accepted came from a grocer who wanted to expand his store and bank account by tearing down an adjacent small apartment building he also owned. "That rent control board," the landlord part of him lamented, "has me by the short hairs, in a real financial bind. I'm prohibited from raising the rates to cover the rising costs of maintenance, property taxes, and other expenses. The snug-as-a-bug tenants have no intentions of moving to comparable, more expensive housing; and I can't find any legal way to evict them. Pretty soon that aging money pit will be draining off *all* my grocery profits."

He figured a fire provided the perfect solution. Not only would it rid him of the pesky tenants, but an insurance company would pay for the store expansion. I agreed, for $5,000, to torch the building and gave Blackie a call. My pal had a world of experience in the arson game—some of his more spectacular blazes had made headlines.

Supplied with duplicate keys for each apartment and the basement, we went in late one morning while everyone was at work. After turning on gas jets in each unit, Blackie soaked the place with a flammable chemical and struck a match.

Looking over my shoulder as we raced for the car, I spotted a figure in a first-floor window, and ran back.

"What the hell you doin'?" Blackie yelled.

I busted the window with my elbow and pulled out a fat yellow striped cat I'd seen frantically clawing and meowing a silent cry for help behind the glass. I set him down on the grass.

"Can't hurt animals, huh?" said Blackie as we sped away. He didn't seem angry, though the delay had placed him in danger, too.

I didn't answer, but later I often wondered about that incident. Would I have gone back for a person? And what kind of person

PROPERTY OF
HIGH POINT PUBLIC LIBRARY
HIGH POINT, NORTH CAROLINA

was I, who didn't hesitate to injure human beings but worried about a cat? I know I was sick, evil sick, a vicious menace, and the crime didn't exist that I wouldn't commit. A wiseguy wanted his cheating girlfriend "roughed up good," and I nearly killed her with my ball-peen hammer. "Break this union guy's legs" was another assignment, and I threw in the fingers as a bonus. Even some Mafiosi got queasy witnessing my savagery. Of course, there are crimes for which the statute of limitations never expires, so I can't write about them.

I didn't fear getting hurt or killed, and perhaps having no concern for my own well-being explains partially why I didn't care about others. The only outcome I vowed I wouldn't accept, which probably traced back to that nightmare in the childhood attic, was being locked away in prison. I deluded myself that matters would never come to that, but I should have known better.

On a Monday morning early in December 1976, I'd just returned to the apartment from closing the after-hours club when a knock sounded on the door. I sneaked a look between the curtains and saw three guys in suits, one holding a walkie-talkie: cops.

"Tell 'em I'm not here," I said to Mary, and headed for the bedroom closet.

It wasn't the cops but the feds, and they'd brought a search warrant. They came in guns drawn, and in less than a minute I felt a cold steel barrel on the nape of my neck. "Back out, pal. Put your hands on your head."

Outside, in handcuffs, I saw a half-dozen FBI men and a like number of Staten Island police. Either it was a slow crime day or they judged me a very bad apple. Never ask a cop nothin' is a good credo, so I could only guess.

But I figured I *knew*, and what went through my mind was escape. I'd be alert every moment for the chance. They had me, had me for a long time, I was sure, on the drugs in Jersey and the cars in Maine, but I'd die before I did time in one of their prisons.

Chapter 8

"What's your occupation, Mr. Minucci?"

"I drive a school bus, Your Honor."

"Do you have a family?"

"A wife and four children, sir."

"How long have you lived at your current address?"

"More than two-and-a-half years, Your Honor."

It had been just three hours since my bust and the ride to Manhattan's Federal Courts Building, but already I stood before a U.S. Magistrate who'd decide if I'd get bail. He asked what I had to say for myself.

"I'm not guilty, sir, though I know that's not what we're here to determine. You say you want to hear about me? I was raised in foster homes, joined the army as a teenager, worked various low-pay jobs in New Jersey after that. Five years ago I moved to Maine with my family and found employment with Diamond International, a large lumber and paper company. We did well in Maine, sir, even bought a little property, but my wife missed her family back here. Also, where we lived was very isolated. I thought the children would benefit from more friends. So we moved again, Your Honor. I'd like to mention that I recently graduated from Staten Island Community College, using the G.I. Bill, for which I'm grateful, and I'm hoping to use the skills I've learned as a layout artist to find work with a newspaper or magazine. I just don't understand these charges, Your Honor," I concluded.

I understood them perfectly well. There were six: (1) fraudulent transference of VIN numbers; (2) theft of motor vehicles; (3) transportation of stolen vehicles across state lines; (4) intent to defraud; (5) sale of stolen vehicles; and (6) interstate flight to avoid prosecution.

The FBI was nowhere to be seen. Evidently they had performed their duty and gone on to other matters. I was in the hands of this magistrate and, by extension, his aging, gray-haired, kindly appearing bailiff. I could have run right then, but I liked the way things had proceeded so far. A *bail* hearing. I could meet any bail the judge set, though a circuitous approach would be needed. It wouldn't look good for Mary to come over and plunk down a shoe box full of cash.

When the judge said "own recognizance," I had to restrain myself from racing out of his court. I'd been popping out of my skin, expecting one of those FBI agents to return and say Maine had requested "a hold" until someone could be sent to pick me up. Or the FBI guy saying, "Your Honor, there are also some serious warrants charging this man in New Jersey."

What *was* going on in Jersey? I'd fled to Maine, uprooting the family, on a cop's word that a bust was imminent. In fact, our house had been raided the Monday morning after we lammed, and Blackie assured me that, as far as he could tell, I was still very much wanted.

Surely, I reasoned, the vaunted FBI hadn't overlooked New Jersey drug warrants when they came to pick me up for Maine. Previously, I'd made no effort to learn my status—what I didn't know couldn't hurt me? But now I had to know. I had to find out what I faced. Gripped with paranoia, I turned the matter over and over in my head. However I viewed it, being released on my own recognizance, with instructions to surrender myself in three weeks at the sheriff's office in Bangor, made no sense.

I reached out to Blackie, as I often did, and he called in a few favors. Blackie discovered that, though the warrants were still outstanding, the cops weren't eager to bring me in. The snitch (a wannabe biker) upon whom they built their case had died. Without him, and without the drugs they had expected to confiscate raiding my house, but didn't, the cops couldn't get a conviction. The charges hadn't been dropped—they hoped something would pop up to revive them—but weren't being pursued.

With just Maine to worry about, I asked around the club, and soon was talking on the phone with a wiseguy-recommended attorney in Bangor. If I had been charged in Montana, the Mob would have known someone there, too. "I'm Frank Minucci," I told the lawyer. "I've got some problems up in your country."

"Frank the Bank!" he enthused.

Frank the Bank?

"That's what the law's been calling you. Big-money mobster who soiled our pristine state."

Oh, man.

"No sweat, buddy. They ain't got anything on you."

"You've investigated my case?"

"Without a retainer? Not a chance. But this call suggests you desire my services. They ain't got anything on any client I represent."

"Good. 'Cause I ain't guilty."

"Right." He coughed. "Look, send Mr. Green up here and I'll see where we stand."

Mr. Green meant money. Usually lawyers use the name when talking to a judge: "Your Honor, I need a continuance until Mr. Green gets here," meaning the attorney is waiting to be paid. Judges understand. They were lawyers once. Speedy justice must not interfere with commerce.

Twenty days later I flew to Maine and caught a cab to the lawyer's office. He was cool. His eyebrows lifted just slightly when he saw me: I wore blue overalls, a torn check shirt, straw hat, and scuffed work boots. I shambled like a loose-jointed yokel, spoke with a Southern drawl, and affected the shyness of a backwoods maiden.

"Frank the Bank," he said.

"Might as well go all the way," I said.

I guessed my mouthpiece's age at thirty-two; a smooth, smiling yuppie, five-feet-ten, a golf and tennis buff, no doubt, in the summer, but best of all, a thorough cynic. This wasn't a guy who thought justice would be served by a client of his, no matter how guilty, doing time.

He drove me to the sheriff's department, where the sheriff himself handed me an arrest card (name, address, birthdate, etc.) and said to fill it out. Although the officer always performs this chore, I said, "It's okay," before my lawyer could protest. The law wanted a handwriting sample to compare with the signature on the back of that check I'd endorsed—left-handed.

I took the pencil the man gave me and started to print like a first-grader. Three minutes and two broken pencil points later, I hadn't gotten through my name. The sheriff grabbed the arrest card, cursing, and said to "have your fun now because we'll have ours later."

Over coffee, before heading back to the airport, I asked my attorney how I stood.

"Okay. Here's the bottom line. The D.A. wants to send you away for five-to-seven."

"Years?"

"It ain't days."

"What do they have?"

"Not much. You want to go over these charges one-by-one?"

What the hell was he thinking? That I didn't care? "Yeah," I said. "Why don't we do that?"

"Okay. First, fraudulent transference of VIN numbers: you're not guilty. It was that guy, what's his name, Ed. Our ace-in-the-hole. He hasn't been charged, and we both know why. The D.A. looks good if he nails a mob guy like you, but he makes too many enemies if he brings in the cops. They got a laundry list of indictments to scare you into a plea."

"What about Number Two?"

"Theft of motor vehicles. They're dreaming. We know what the plural is, but they can't prove it, at least not without dirtying their own. I don't know, but I suspect you ran a lot of stolen cars. Whatever, that's what the D.A. thinks. Only they can't prove it, so you're not guilty."

"How's that?"

"You know someone named Zeal?"

"Yeah."

"They traced a call you made to him from your mobile home."

I remembered. One time I'd gotten lazy, over-confident, and hadn't driven to a pay phone. *Stupid,* I thought, but out loud I said, "Yeah?"

"The number you called was no longer in service, but they knew it belonged to this guy Zeal. There was only one Zeal in the current listings, so they phoned him. Turns out he's a homicide detective."

I returned the yuppie's questioning stare till he lowered his eyes. The D.A. had reached Blackie's brother, a cop, in the honesty department the polar opposite of my friend. But I wasn't going to tell the lawyer about any of the Zeals.

"You see what that meant," said the mouthpiece. "They figure anyone dealing with a homicide detective is well connected. He's operating a ring. He's stealing vehicles, plural. They can't prove it, though, so you're not guilty."

"Number Three."

"Transportation of stolen vehicles across state lines. Not guilty. They need Ed to testify but they don't dare call him."

I liked the way this was going.

"Intent to defraud. Not guilty again. They can't prove what you *intended.*"

"You got good news on Five and Six?"

"They're a little stickier."

"What do you mean by that?"

"They've got you dead to rights, Frank. Sale of stolen vehicles. Forget that plural. You *did* sell the pickup to the undercover guy. Doesn't matter if you say you had no idea it was hot. Then there's interstate flight. No way we're gonna beat that one."

Two weeks later I was back in Maine, again clad as "Harry Hillbilly," to eyeball a meeting between the D.A. and my mouthpiece. The upshot: If I'd plead to a pair of felonies, the state would recommend two years. They had me, all right, but chances were good that plenty of dirty linen would get aired at the trial.

The D.A. talked tough, but I wondered. He seemed genuinely

to believe that I was a high-ranking mobster, and it made him nervous. A plan began to form in my head.

When I returned in three weeks for trial, the D.A.'s darkest suspicions were confirmed. I wore a handmade suit, silk shirt and tie, a $300 pair of shoes, and sported three large diamond rings. Lending "moral support" were a pair of five-foot-nine, 340-pound bookends I called "my friends." Actually, they were Geno and Butchie, two guys in the moving business. They had instructions to keep quiet, "look normal," which meant they'd terrify anyone with eyes. When either moved, it appeared his suit would burst at the seams.

The judge, a thin, bearded guy, wanted to know if "the sides" had reached an agreement; in other words, a plea, to save the People time, money, and perhaps embarrassment.

"No, Your Honor," said the D.A. "We're prepared to proceed to trial."

"No, Your Honor," said my lawyer, "and that's a shame. My client is a property holder in Maine." I'd bought 6 ½ acres near the mobile home when I thought we might need more room for the stolen car caper. "My client is a family man. He's a college graduate with professors willing to attest to his character. I can call his parish priest to vouch for him.

"What does the prosecution have? Two witnesses, at best, undercover police officers who bought a stolen pickup from Mr. Minucci. My client violated the letter of the law, but not its spirit. He didn't know that pickup was stolen. He was doing a favor for his friend Ed. When we call Ed . . ." He let the thought hang in the air. "But let's talk about the lack of witnesses. No witnesses means . . ."

The D.A. was on his feet, face livid, hands shaking, barely able to contain himself. "Counsel wants witnesses?" he seethed. "I have a subpoena for the best witness of all. An individual who knows the truth about Frank the Bank Minucci. An individual who will testify truthfully, I guarantee, or face perjury charges. That individual is the defendant's wife, Mrs. Mary Minucci!"

Where did this come from? A wife couldn't be forced to testify against her husband. I doubted torture could unseal Mary's lips.

The D.A. had given me the perfect opening for what I'd

planned, and I came to my feet with a loud scrape of chair. "Mr. Prosecutor," I said in my best gangster voice. "If you put my wife on the stand, I promise you'll regret it. I'll come over this railing and rip your eyes out!"

The judge was gaveling for order, but I had more to say. The bailiff hadn't made a move. He had his gaze on Geno and Butchie, who stared back placidly.

"I don't know how you do things in Maine," I continued, never taking my eyes off the D.A., "but in New York, and especially in Italian families, we don't get our loved ones involved. You mess with my wife, you'll be sucking up moose crap from six feet under, I promise you that."

The judge called a recess when I sat down, and he, my attorney, and the prosecutor met in his chambers. We had a new deal when they emerged: I'd plead guilty to one felony—sale of a stolen vehicle—and be remanded to New York for two years' probation. My lawyer said the D.A. huffed and puffed about "threats to officers of the court," but didn't offer spirited resistance when His Honor urged a settlement. I figure they didn't pay that prosecutor enough to test whether I'd been bluffing.

"That was some show," the lawyer said when we were back in his office. "You had me going.

"Now, let's talk about my fee."

"What do you think I owe you?"

He could have just said nine thousand dollars, but of course had to make a production of adding up hours, at $150 per, on a desk calculator. He never seemed to make a phone call shorter than an hour, and "preparation of motions"—a job performed by his $80-a-week secretary—took much longer than one would have thought.

"So you liked what I did in court," I said, holding his bill in my lap.

"Loved it. A real cute scam."

"Then you're gonna go plum wild over this next move."

I leaned across his desk, picked up his phone, and dialed a number. "Ed," I said, when my former partner answered, "this is Frank the Bank."

"Frank?" I didn't think so much fear could be squeezed into a single word.

"We need to talk, Ed. I want you to drive into Bangor and meet me at this coffee shop."

"Talk about what?"

"And bring forty-five hundred dollars. I got my lawyer right here, and he'll tell you my legal bill is twice that. I'm only chargin' you half."

"But . . ."

"Be there in forty-five minutes, buddy, be on time, or I'll come out to *your* place. I just got two years for our deal, and you walked away clean. No way was that fair to me. I coulda ruined you in that courtroom. It's time you do the right thing."

"Okay, okay. I guess that's fair."

"You're gettin' a bargain."

"Amazin'," the lawyer said when I put down the phone. I wonder what he said when I didn't return to his office with the money.

I enjoyed champagne on the flight back to Newark, drove to the Brighton Avenue Club, and accepted congratulations. I thought I might play a few hands of blackjack—surely this was my day—but it was a lose-lose situation: If I won, the boss wouldn't like it, and if I lost, *I* wouldn't.

Anger and surprise were also my reactions when I arrived home early the next morning. Mary and two of her ex–Jersey boyfriends were having a party; at least that's how I interpreted the combination of loud talk, dancing, laughter, booze, and rock music. The only cause for celebration I could think of was their belief I'd gone to jail.

I went ballistic, breaking the door down. The boyfriends, frozen by the dramatic entrance, took turns getting punched and kicked. In my fury, I grabbed one of them by the back of his hair and slammed his face into the hardwood floor. At last I threw them out the door—they weren't the ones I wanted to kill—and turned to Mary cowering in a corner.

I'd been a cuckold before, which would have made me a laughingstock if the wiseguys knew, and had warned my wife, in tones she couldn't fail to comprehend, that I wouldn't stand for it again.

My mind, my whole body, became engulfed in a dark rage, a murderous fury. I moved toward Mary, feeling strangely in control, but not. I felt unstoppable.

"Daddy," I heard a voice say. That's what saved Mary, the one word, "Daddy," and the memory it triggered, vivid enough to penetrate my wall of hatred and anger. I remembered my father Carmine, his features contorted, pointing the gun at Lucille; and my mother, face battered and bloody. Most important I remembered myself, how helpless I was, wishing they could just get along.

"It's over," I said to Mary. "I'm leaving you and not coming back. That's better than killing you."

I spent the night driving around Staten Island, gulping coffee in all-night cafés, reading classified ads when the first newspaper hit the stands. Soon as I figured the landlord should be stirring, I headed for the Port Richmond section of northwest Staten Island and rented a furnished room. The room wasn't much, though the owner was proud of it, and I said, "Yeah, yeah, yeah," as he laid down the house rules. I paid rent for two months, which he liked, and drove back to what I already considered Mary's place. In my haste to leave and avoid murdering her, I'd forgotten something.

The money. Sullen and cowed, she watched me go for the shoe boxes, not saying a word. Both of us knew, I think, that better-late-than-never applied to the finish of our disastrous union. I laid a wad of hundred-dollar bills on the coffee table, said there'd be more when the family needed it, and that the furniture and other stuff was hers. She never spoke the whole time.

We even got a divorce, using lawyers and all, which went without a hitch. She knew better than to mess matters up with a court-mandated settlement, and besides I was more generous than a judge would have been. Visitation rights, she understood, were whenever I wanted them. I said I hoped she'd remarry, and that boyfriends had nothing to fear from me.

I immersed myself in the criminal life. The money flowed at the after-hours club, and my honest counts didn't go unnoticed by important wiseguys. Soon I was loansharking on a regular basis, collecting vig (interest), running a numbers operation, and selling dope. At the end of each week I delivered the money to rough characters named Vinnie, Steve, and Cousin Mitch.

Weird requests were commonplace, and since there was very little I wouldn't do to impress the wiseguys and earn money for myself, they often got aimed my way. "Frankie," said one of my bosses, drinking himself into oblivion at the club. "I need you to do a job. I'll pay two grand."

"What's that?"

"I want a bullet put in my worthless stepson's head. Know what that clown did?"

"What?"

"Threatened my life. Right in front of his wife, who I respect. Then he set fire to my car."

I waited for more.

"Will you do it?"

"Sure. When?"

This wasn't the kind of guy you tried to talk out of something. You didn't ask, "Are you sure? He's your stepson, you might want to think this over." If he wanted somebody whacked, he meant it.

"We'll leave right now," he said. "I'll drive you over there and wait while you do it."

I picked up the paper bag I kept under the bar and followed him out. When we arrived at the stepson's home, I donned the leather gloves and ski mask the bag contained, and removed my .38. Then I headed for the front door.

The wife answered my 3 A.M. ring. This is a woman the guy respects, I thought, not a fact to be taken lightly, but what could I do? I grabbed her neck in a one-handed vise and knocked her nearly unconscious with a blow to the head from the pistol butt. I hurried through the house, room by room, but the stepson wasn't home. The wife had shakily staggered upright as I left. "No cops," I said, "or you'll be as dead as your old man when I find him."

I told the boss what happened as he drove back to the club, expecting him to lose what little control he had. Like many gangsters, and with some it's a bluff, he always seemed right on the brink.

It turned out I was like gold in his eyes. When I mentioned the young woman he "respected" and the knot on her head, he said it served her right, what did she expect, marrying someone like his stepson?

I'm glad the guy wasn't home. As usually happens, the family became good friends again, everything forgotten. Till now, the stepson never knew it was me who nearly punched his clock, and since we're still good pals, I guess I'm forgiven.

Some of the people I worked for can only be described as unstable. Or maybe that's how they wanted me to view them: keep him off-balance and guessing. One night a boss came in, mean and drunk, and started loudly insulting the customers. He owned the joint, what the hell, so I had to look the other way.

Then he turned on me.

I'd been standing at the far end of the bar, talking with a female friend, and saw him lurching in our direction. "You're a low-life," he said, his sweaty face up against mine.

"Take it easy," I said.

"Who's the boss?"

A childish question. I played along.

"You are."

"Right! And people like you are a dime a dozen."

"If you say so."

"That's right. I'm the boss." He wheeled around, almost falling, and announced to his customers, "I do whatever I want," he said and to prove it he overturned a table.

"I oughta teach you a lesson," he said loudly, blurrily focusing back on me.

"Maybe tomorrow," I said. "Not tonight. Tonight I'm gonna throw you out if you don't cool down."

What I said didn't register. Not right away. He noticed my female friend, a pretty blonde, and by way of introduction grabbed for a breast. She pulled away. He said, "This guy you're with's a bum. I got what you need," and lunged for her again.

I threw a glass of scotch in his face, but instead of jarring him into temporary sanity, it caused him to reach for a stool to club me with. Gianni from the 4 O'Clock Lounge saved the boss's life. Lightning-quick, I whipped out my gun and had the barrel to his temple, a real Billy the Kid move, and in my rage I pulled the trigger. But Gianni was even faster. He got his finger between the hammer and firing pin.

"You . . ." the boss began.

"Shut up!" I said.

"You . . ."

"Look at it this way," Gianni said coolly, staring the boss right in the eye. "This has been the luckiest day of your life."

I was finished at the Brighton Avenue Club, but other wiseguys had noticed me and liked me. Not that "liking" had a lot to do with anything—I'd proven myself as an earner, and thus received offers from various crews. I chose Big Sal's. Often a guy called "Big" is little, and vice versa, but Big Sal was not misnamed: he stood a solid six-two, all beefy muscle—a hard character with an explosive temper. Since I was a similar type, he said we'd get along fine.

If there was a buck to be made, Sal had his hand in it. Drugs. Bookmaking. Numbers. Loansharking. Customers who borrowed money from him learned that no matter how much they paid back, it seemed they still owed more. I'd done work for Sal before—the beating of Junebug an example—but never full-time.

Sal operated from a local bar where each week I delivered cash to him from various dope dealers I "ran." Not long after I joined his crew, in July 1977, one of the dealers came up short for the week. I knew I'd get the money, probably have to rearrange the dealer's face a little, to teach a lesson, but Big Sal was livid. Nobody stole from him! He pointed a gun at *me,* and a killer named Ray held a knife to my face.

Long before, death had ceased to hold much fear for me. In fact, I often thought I'd had a longer life than I could rightly expect. "Tell him to do a good job," I said, "because if I'm alive, I'll come straight after your family. I'll leave you for last."

Big Sal laughed. "You got some serious courage," he decided, and motioned Ray to back off. "But I want my money," he added. "Next week at the latest."

The fact is, Big Sal treated everybody poorly. He ruled by intimidation, and his pockets were never full enough. I learned, though it took some time, that I stood in no danger at all. I ranked

as Sal's top earner, and he didn't want to risk losing production
that included moving 3,000 hits of THC each week.

I made good money working for Sal—two thousand a week—
but my personal life was on the skids. At the finish of long days
I could choose between visiting after-hours clubs with other members of the crew, or returning alone to that dismal room I rented.
Too often I selected the route of the clubs, where increasingly the
drug of choice was no longer booze, but marijuana or THC.

Everyone smoked or took hits. You were suspect if you didn't,
out of place, not "one of the boys."

I started using speed again. Whenever Blackie called, the one
guy who could have relieved the increasing loneliness and depres-
sion I felt, I said I was too busy to see him.

Blackie would have known what I was doing, and I couldn't
face his disappointment.

Chapter 9

Late in November 1977, I sat in the office of John Sanders, director of security for a large department store (actually, two huge and separate buildings, one a grocery supermarket). Sanders, a former New York City police officer much decorated for his work on the Rescue Squad, represented everything I did not: decency, service to the community, selflessness, things like that.

The hardest heart had to admire John Sanders. He had risked his life time and again to save citizens trapped in collapsed buildings, pinned in wrecked cars, stranded in stalled subway trains or elevators. Sanders adopted a troubled teenager he talked out of a suicide during his work on the Rescue Squad. Now, besides his duties at the store, he volunteered time as a scoutmaster.

This do-gooder—in the best sense of the word—needed help, and I could tell he'd turned to me as a last resort. The store was located on the north shore of Staten Island adjacent to an apartment complex not *quite* as threatening as some in the South Bronx and Bedford-Stuyvesant, but close. Individuals and gangs of toughs terrorized decent residents, forcing people to live behind barred doors, their lives in danger if they ventured outside. Gunshots rang out day and night. The cops never visited the community after dark (too dangerous), and car patrols, not foot patrols (which might have done some good), were the best residents could expect in daytime.

Sanders told me that the environment at the store, which abutted the ghetto, was fast becoming identical to the apartment complex. If a customer were lucky enough to reach the store (savage muggings and purse snatchings were common), she had to feel like a fool to pay for anything. Shoplifting had reached epidemic proportions.

"What about your security force?" I asked.

"You know what those guys get paid?" Sanders said.

"What?" I said.

"Not enough to challenge these thugs. A few tried and got stomped. Frank, people need this store. But it's not going to be here long—the owners will *have* to move—unless it can be made safe."

"What do you want from me?" I asked. "If money is your problem, get tougher security guards."

"Don't you get it?" he said. "These are rent-a-cops, looking to subsidize their office salaries so they can send their kids to camp. They aren't tough enough. They sure aren't dedicated enough. I've stayed up nights thinking on this, and then thought some more. I believe we need someone like you."

I studied the five-foot-nine, clean-cut Sanders, still trim with a trace of college kid good looks. I would have laughed at most anybody else, but I know Sanders meant it.

"Here's what I'll do," I said. "I'll go see somebody. Find out if this can be worked out."

The "somebody" I saw was Howie, a black loanshark and numbers runner who reputedly had clout in the ghetto. Howie knew I had connections and was eager to help, but right away he said nothing could be done. A "leader" he might be, but the gangs and toughs didn't listen to anybody. "Frank," he said, "they're not scared of the mob, the cops, or the devil himself."

Before going back to Sanders, I spent an hour checking out the store. The former Rescue Squad cop hadn't exaggerated at all. Harrowing encounters awaited customers in the parking lot; if lucky enough to make it inside, they found themselves in shoplifter's heaven. Most of the thieves at least tried to conceal what they stole under a coat or inside a pocket, but a few, the wave of the future if something weren't done, just helped themselves to whatever they wanted.

"What do you think?" Sanders asked, when I sat once again in his office.

"I can handle it," I said.

"You sure you got the time for this, Frank? What are you doing these days?"

Sanders really was a straight shooter. Did he expect me to say that currently I worked for mobsters? That I ran numbers, loansharked, collected vig, and dragged late-payers down the street tied to the bumper of my car? All he knew was my tough-guy reputation.

"I got the time," I said, "to do a good deed."

Actually, I wanted to put some distance between me and the whole mob scene, at least for a while. I envisioned the store job as a lark.

I told Sanders he needed to let me hire five people. "Two hundred bucks a week per guy," I said. "Three hundred a week for me."

"Okay," Sanders said.

"We'll carry handcuffs, badges, and guns. My people will like that."

"Agreed," Sanders said. "But I hope you'll exercise some restraint."

"Trust me."

It took less than an afternoon to round up the five guys I wanted, and on December 1, 1977, I gathered my security force in the store's parking lot. "We don't want to be too gentle about this," I said unnecessarily. "The idea is to scare these low-lifes away. Show 'em they're not welcome here. Don't kill nobody, unless you got to, and once you've delivered the message, you need to call the cops. Let's do it right and kick some ass."

Out in the parking lot, a cold wind blowing, we violated one of Sanders' cardinal rules: You need to catch them before you "warn" them. One of my men spotted a guy he said looked "suspicious" heading for the main entrance. He rushed up to the man, said, "Take your business elsewhere," and scored a one-punch knockout. For good measure he kicked the unconscious guy in the ribs and added, "Don't come back."

Wiseguys liked to brag, "There weren't no break-ins or muggings where Carlo Gambino lived," and later the same truth applied to John Gotti's environs, a major reason his neighbors supported him.

We operated on the same principle: Savage reprisals, no mercy.

Bedlam reigned at the store, for days. Each morning we fanned through the store, taking up preassigned positions, and then stomping people we caught stealing. None of us wore a uniform, and badges, handcuffs, and guns were kept concealed. We weren't on duty to prevent shoplifting, but to punish when it occurred.

Two guys lurked in the parking lot, alert for muggers and purse snatchers. The Staten Island police became fixtures at the store, picking up thieves and more violent types we'd already subdued. The cops never said anything, but I know they liked our style.

The best part was when somebody fought back, a not infrequent occurrence. As the loanshark, Howie had said, these were characters who respected no one, and it helped the morale of my crew when we got challenged. We *loved* to fight.

December 7, 1977, has to rank as one of the two most important days of my life; perhaps *the* most important, because without that day the second event probably would never have occurred.

It started in ludicrous fashion. I crouched on hands and knees in the men's department beneath a rack of clothes peering between winter coats at a guy in the nearby hardware department. He was eying some wrenches in a manner indicating he'd soon steal them. The moment they vanished into his big overcoat pocket I intended to fly at him like Giants linebacker Sam Huff, build a head of steam, blast him to the floor, and pound him until I tired of it, which usually took a long time.

At the same time, unknown to me, a saleswoman in the shoe department was also witnessing what she thought was a theft, or worse, and called security. Two of my men happened to be working inside this day and answered her summons.

"What's the problem?"

"Look over there," she said, pointing to the men's department. "There's a strange man crawling around in the coats."

Ready to kill—all my security guys had become imbued with a crusader's fervor to rid the store of outside thieves—they stormed over to the coat rack. One guy shoved his hands into my back pockets and yanked me into the aisle, just as I saw the wrenches vanishing into the guy's overcoat.

"What are you maniacs doing?" I yelled.

"Geez, Frank, we didn't know it was you."

"Don't you look before you act?"

"It was this lady in shoes. She thought you were a thief. C'mon, I'll show you. It happened 'cause of her."

"I don't want to meet the lady in shoes."

"Might not be a bad idea," said Piazza, our history scholar. Thumbing the moth-eaten lapels of his Salvation Army thrift store jacket (dressed to blend in, we looked as scruffy as the people we busted), he added, "We don't exactly look like store dicks, and this could happen again. Remember, Sanders wanted us to introduce ourselves to his regular help."

"Okay, okay," I said. "Take me to the old bag."

When the 600-pound wall of ushering muscle halted and parted, my mouth dropped wide open. Standing in front of me was the most beautiful young woman I'd ever laid eyes on—a petite five feet, perfectly proportioned with big brown eyes, raven hair, and the face of an angel. I searched for celebrity comparisons, a habit of mine, and instantly put together a combination that lasted: a cross between Liz Taylor, Natalie Wood, and Betty Boop. For me, it was love at first sight. As if trapped in the freeze-frame of a hokey boy-meets-girl TV commercial with exploding fireworks, chirping lovebirds, and violin music, I stood motionless, slack-jawed, stunned by her beauty.

"This is Frank Minucci," I heard someone say. "He's the chief goon around here."

"I didn't know," she said, and began to laugh.

Thinking she was making fun of me, I stupidly felt compelled to defend myself, and the first thing out of my mouth was wrong: "Because of you, a thief got away."

"Well, I'm sorry," she said. "You should have told me who you are. You scared me, skulking down there on the floor."

"What's your name?" I asked, attempting to rally, while the sight of her rolled my mind and stomach in turmoil. I'd never met a woman like this. Biker girls and the types who hung around with mobsters had been my speed. Not someone with a shining angel face.

For a moment I didn't think she'd tell me. But I suppose she figured I could find out. "Patty Joy Naimo," she said, and the name, like everything else, seemed perfect.

Patty Joy Naimo, I love you, I thought. Out loud I asked, "Will you have a cup of coffee with me?"

She didn't answer.

When my second request to have coffee drew no reply, I nodded and headed disconsolately toward another part of the store.

But not for long. I switched surveillance posts with another man and stationed myself near the shoe department—more correctly, near Patty. While I stood around like a lovesick puppy stealing glimpses of her, unwatched shoplifters quickened their pilferage to looters' pace and stole blind the area I'd designated myself to protect.

Patty paid no attention to my stares, but Sanders did. "I'm gonna let you go, and her, too," he said, "if you don't start doing your job."

I had to change tactics. I started writing poems to her, leaving them near the cash register and other places where she couldn't miss them. Whenever she was due a break, I asked her to have coffee. She never said no. She never said anything. I figured I'd wear her down eventually.

Early in January 1978, I finally heard the words I wanted from Patty when I invited her to the food stand: "Okay. Coffee. That's all."

"I don't love you or nothing but I like you a lot," I stated awkwardly while trying to steady the containers I held. A lie, of course. I was so crazy in love that just being near her started my pulse racing and my heart pounding. Shortness of breath. Plus, the real me was very shy, especially around civilized people, and painfully aware of the uncouth image I projected. I feared she'd view me as an offensive baboon.

I masked my tough guy persona that first day, and for hundreds of days that followed, hoping possibly she might learn to love me. Patty seemed to me a dream, "the girl from the other side of the tracks" who, for a thug like me, it was an honor just to be seen with.

Somehow I persuaded her to go on a real date, then another, and although I did most of the talking (she was a great listener), I managed to learn a few things about her. She was twenty-six years old to my thirty-six; had a sixteen-month-old son, Salvatore; and like me, was waiting for a divorce to become final. After her mother had died in childbirth, Patty, a brother, and three sisters, were raised by her father, a postman, and her grandmother. She'd been a nonrebellious, very obedient child and an A student at Port Richmond High School.

The more I got to know Patty, the more I wanted her to love me. She was honorable and honest to a fault, her word as good as gold. Her life, despite the pending divorce, was genuinely stable and organized to a tee. She paid bills on time, never missed appointments, and kept her small house white-gloves clean. She worried more about the needs of others than her own. Except for possibly Mom Klein, I'd never met a woman who took such pride in herself and her surroundings.

I was obsessed with Patty. I lived to be with her, talked about her to everyone, bought her flowers daily, and showered her with presents I hoped adequately expressed my love. Instead of catching bad guys at the store, I spent my time daydreaming, or writing love notes and poetry.

As January drew to a close, Sanders had become less concerned about me doing my job. We'd virtually eliminated the formerly rampant shoplifting, made the parking lot safe, and honest, relaxed shoppers again filled the store. Of course, actual theft wasn't down: the crew and I stole more than the boosters ever had, but that would cease when our job was judged complete.

My problem with Patty was never being able to tell her the truth. The job ended in mid-February, and I had no visible means of support. Yet I always had plenty of money to spend and she naturally became curious. "I paint houses," I said, which if true would have made me the highest paid house painter in history, given the presents I lavished on her. Truth was, I'd gone back to taking numbers and collecting debts, my specialty.

Patty was always totally honest with me, yet I needed to be 100 percent dishonest with her, inventing ever more fantastic explanations for the large amounts of money I had. I could have cooled it with the cash, I suppose, but then what reason would justify dating her? Obviously, I didn't have a clue.

"You're a good person," Patty told me. "I see many positive qualities in you struggling to get out. I wish you'd let me help."

But I couldn't. I was sure I'd lose her. The unbroken string of bad things in my life continued, and even my angel Patty, I convinced myself, couldn't deal with them. I saw only goodness in her, a naive product of a sheltered background incapable of even conceiving of some of the deeds I'd done.

By gentle, persistent questioning, however, she did elicit that I'd largely been raised by Mom and Pop Klein. Eventually, I took Patty to meet the Kleins, and she learned a good deal about my wretched childhood directly from Mom Klein.

Patty became friends with Mom and Pop Klein, who could only tell about my life up to the mid-teens. Through her, the Kleins and I were reunited and remained close until their deaths a few years ago. During this period I began appreciating Pop Klein, a decent man who worked hard all his life and put his money on the table at the end of each week. But I couldn't be like Pop, I told myself, because I thought I needed bags of money to hold on to Patty.

I felt great having Patty on my arm at fancy restaurants and nightclubs, and she introduced me to museums, my first adult taste of a culture higher than wiseguy after-hours joints. We began taking long romantic weekends to small towns in Vermont, New Hampshire, and the Pennsylvania Amish country. On shorter day-trips we took Salvatore along with us for picnics in quaint parks and shopping in flea markets.

Gently, always gently, Patty found buried pieces of me that she interpreted as decent. "Struggling to get out," she repeated.

The only toys I ever had, a tin duck and car, were given to me to keep me quiet while imprisoned in the attic.

Partying with Frankie Famular, "Frankie Fame," led to me opening my own nightclub at age 22.

Customized bike,
my pride and joy.

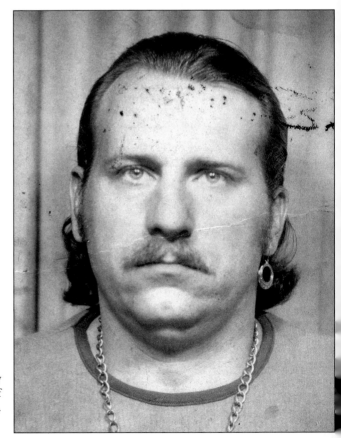

A photo of me after my
election as president of
the Nomads.

Nomad vice-president Shades (*left*) and president Frenchy.

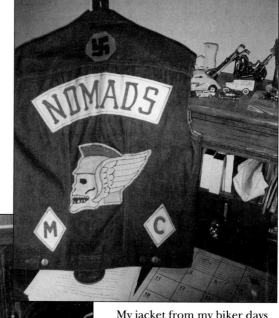

My jacket from my biker days with the Nomads.

Behind wheel of camper. "Drug store to the hippies," 1968.

Jay, second oldest son, in
front of "Porky Pig" that
blazed a trail to Maine
in 1972.

In rural Maine with the 1968
GTO used to elude the cops.

Patty, "The Lady in Shoes,"
and Frank, "The Chief
Goon," on the lap of Major's
store Santa, Christmas 1978.

How I looked when Patty reported me as a "strange man crawling around in the coats."

Wedding Day—behind the bride and groom are (*from left*) ring bearer Jay, Pop Klein, and Big Phil.

Patty and me with Mom
and Pop Klein on our
wedding day.

Blackie Zeal and his wife,
Barbara, who helped me
break my addiction to speed.

Angelo, age 2, displaying
Daddy's drug money.

From left: Keith, Salvatore,
Candice, Angelo, and Patty.

Angelo and me, 1984.

My bathroom before my first
out-of-body experience.
My life was reduced to
snorting cocaine off the
back of my toilet.

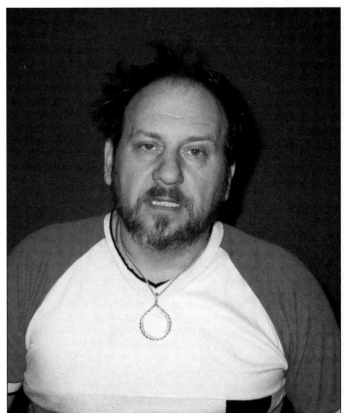

Snapshot of a wasted cokehead taken by one of the
Sixpack two weeks before
out-of-body experience.

Shedding the old—Minucci and Pastor Paul McCarthy destroy $1.4 million worth of birth and baptismal certificates during 1985 church service.

Rev. Don Swantek and me.

Talking with Pat Robertson on "700 Club" in 1986.

With Dr. Norman Vincent Peale. Dr. Peale told my story in *Guide Post* magazine.

Street minister in action in Bedford-Stuyvesant recruiting high school dropouts to study for GED.

The Christmas party for underprivileged children we give every year in Newark, New Jersey.

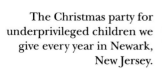

As a traveling preacher in Panama Beach, Florida.

In Florida with Ralph Marinacci, an executive with the Full Gospel Fellowship Businessmen's International.

Delivering sermon at ChristWay Church, Kenilworth.

My sister Shirley with her daughter. I hadn't seen her in thirty years, then she saw my HBO special and we reunited.

Patty's parents, Anna and Tony Naimo. Tony taught me how to be a father.

With sons, Ronnie (*left*) and
Jay, 1994.

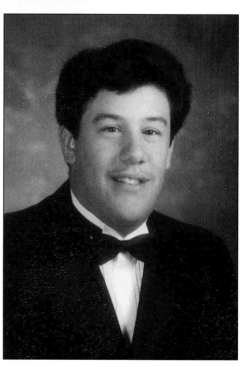

My son, Salvatore, age 18.

My son, Angelo, age 16.

My role as "Tony T" in *Carlito's Way*
was the last I'll ever do involving profanity.

With Bill Cosby. I played a bartender in a 1995 "Cosby Mysteries" episode.

NBA commercial with Houston Rockets players (*from left*) Hakeem
Olajuwon, Sam Cassell, Kenny Smith, Otis Thorpe.

With Bob Jacobs, the paramedic who brought me back to life. Without this
man's skills, there would be no book. Thanks, Bobby.

Patty and me at Pallace's Resort, Catskills, New York.

PROPERTY OF
HIGH POINT PUBLIC LIBRARY
HIGH POINT, NORTH CAROLINA

Clearly she cared about me as no one had, and I loved her warmth, sensitivity and intelligence. But she was, truth to tell, *naive*. Patty at times clung to me like a child, claiming I gave her strength; not so, it was she who made *me* strong, in the long haul.

I found it amazing how two completely different personalities meshed so well. I, a dishonest and vicious predator, believed there were no unbreakable rules. Patty, conversely, played fair and square and expected others to do the same. That I couldn't do. I felt that to know me was to hate me, so I hid behind a forest of deceptions and lies. All I had to offer was love, and I thought that wouldn't be enough.

Throughout my life I'd defined love in acts of sex and extravagant gifts. Patty tried to teach me that love involved being held tenderly in the arms of someone who cared and comforted. All I'd known was distrust and hands that hurt, but Patty's touch soothed and healed. With positive, strengthening words, she kept coming to me with outstretched arms.

I loved her so much, but I didn't know how to show it or how to accept her kindness and nurturing. I knew I should trust her completely, but shame and fear bubbled up when I tried. I was terrified of her hurting me or laughing at me, of her saying I was a chump and all this a game. *She's up to something,* my sick mind warned.

Actually, she was getting too close to me, and I feared what she'd find. I went through episodes of jealousy, played macho games, even behaved cruelly. She'd sit and talk to me, put my head in her lap, rub my face, and try verbally to walk me through the locked torture chambers of my mind. But I wouldn't talk about the nightmares—my parents, the rapes in the attic, the dozen and more foster homes—because I wanted to forget those times I'd been so weak. Maybe they had been my fault, and I was ashamed.

Patty took me to meet her father and stepmother, Anthony and Anna, an event I'd dreaded and postponed as long as possible. They were exactly what I expected: utterly decent, caring people. Anthony Naimo, more streetwise than his sheltered daughter, quickly pegged me a more likely candidate for a police lineup than *any* woman's dreamboat selection for marriage, but he treated me politely, in deference to Patty. He could tell, by reading my speech patterns and body language, that my past was badly checkered, at best. I thanked lucky stars for his inability to know the true *depths* of my degradation.

Early in our courtship, I, the ardent suitor dubious of my masquerade's longevity, tried in beat-the-clock frenzy to keep my intended bedazzled and constantly entertained—hoping to buy an appropriate amount of time to pop the question before she got wise to me. I started warming her to the idea with unsubtle hints, "Wouldn't it be nice not to leave after saying good night?" and "Salvatore needs a strong father figure." Getting nowhere, I finally said, "Patty, marry me."

"We can't," she replied.

"Why not?" I feared the worst.

"Frank, aren't you forgetting something? We're already married, at least in the eyes of the law."

"A mere technicality, my little chickadee," I said in my best W. C. Fields cigar-flicking impersonation that brought out her beautiful smile.

"Seriously," she said. "I think we need more time. So we can get to know each other better."

Precisely what I didn't want, but so it went, initially. However, when our divorces were stamped official, Patty pressed for a wedding date, and I became reluctant. Perhaps the persistent "good person" reminders started me thinking like one. I considered, what were the chances of our growing old happily together?

Very slim, I thought.

I'd either break her heart or get killed. Most of my best friends were dead already, or in prison, and the odds were bound to catch up with me. Even if I survived, our liaison would become the Marriage from Hell—just like my first.

I began stalling on a wedding date, taking secret satisfaction in my perceived role as martyr. But I wasn't sacrificing enough to let her go entirely. Nonetheless, the two times she pushed me into a commitment, I found excuses to postpone.

Tired of confronting what she thought were prenuptial cold feet, Patty confronted me. "Frank, I love you more than life itself, but—"

Cutting her off before the other shoe fell, I kissed her and said,

"I love you too, sweetheart. You're the sun, moon, and stars that light—"

"Hold it!" she said, putting her hand over my mouth. "This time the softsoap won't work. No more sidetracks. No more delays. We either set a definite date or break it off."

Break it off? I'd have chosen a bullet in my head over never seeing Patty again. I hemmed and hawed but she meant business. I agreed to a June 16, 1979, wedding, and the bride-to-be happily began making preparations.

As Patty and her sisters chose her dress, met with the florist, attended wedding showers, and mailed out invitations, I increasingly feared we were making a mistake. My demons were formless, unarticulated (I didn't want to talk or even think about them), but they had made me an almost-empty vessel constructed of stone containing only a heart-crushing feeling of loneliness and rejection. I was a monster and knew it: bitter, cruel, angry, spiteful. I desperately stumbled through life offending and hurting people, constantly doing the wrong thing, a self-gratifying threat to society. My trophies—my life "accomplishments"—came in the form of revenge or reeking devastation, whether stealing, maiming, raping, or torture: the greater the crime, the more I'd been addicted to it.

Was this what a "good person" would bring to Patty?

I remembered as a young man getting sent by a judge to a renowned psychiatrist and head of a mental health clinic in New Jersey. He and his associates determined I was "a mass murderer in the making." The treatment ended when he asked, "Did you ever have intercourse with your mother?" He meant social intercourse, the normal give-and-take between mother and child, but I interpreted his question in a sexual context, leaped up, and began choking him. I would have killed him if his colleagues hadn't pulled me off.

Despite the front I showed Patty, my criminal activities had continued—they hadn't even tapered off. The trick to living two lives—like the key to Lindbergh's solo transatlantic flight—involved getting by without much sleep.

Chapter 10

Besides performing my regular chores for a wiseguy named Frankie, I remained available as the wedding date approached for any additional jobs that might come along. Sure enough, one did: A former state cop named Jackie Tudor wanted his home in upstate New York burned down. This was right up Blackie Zeal's alley, so I subcontracted the work to him.

After collecting from the insurance company, Tudor suggested we use his $50,000 windfall to enter the cocaine business. "How about it?" he asked. "You got the connections?"

"Yeah. But I want to bring my friend Blackie into the deal." I needed somebody I could trust, and this ex–state cop didn't fill the bill. Moreover, he acted as if I were a lowlife criminal, while he was merely a shrewd businessman in search of unorthodox profits.

"Fine by me," said Tudor. "After the first fifty thousand dollars in sales pays back my original investment, we'll cut the pie into thirds." Tudor, I learned, looked to build enough cash to open a fancy private investigator's office.

The three of us flew to Miami, rented a car, and drove to Key West. I met with a guy I'd known in New Jersey, now big in the Florida drug business, who sold us two kilos (4.4 pounds) of coke and 95 pounds of pot for $50,000. On the street, the coke would sell for $200,000 and the marijuana for $40,000. We would split $190,000, after Tudor recouped his investment.

We tasted the coke, sampled the grass, and prepared to leave. My friend had arranged—at a cost of 3½ grams of pure cocaine—for a Key West police officer to escort us to Seventeen Mile Bridge, the link to the mainland. Ripoffs of drug dealers were a major business in Florida and the cop, in his patrol car, lent needed security.

What followed was an under-the-speed-limit drive north to Staten Island. In South Carolina I was resting in the backseat while Tudor drove and Blackie rode shotgun. Evidently Tudor thought I was asleep, and called me "white trash" to my friend. Now that he had his own contact, he said, he'd be cutting me out of future dealings.

Blackie glanced back, saw I was awake, and made neutral sounds which prompted Tudor to go on. The former cop kept badmouthing me as a mindless thug, a "street guy" in over my head with a sophisticated mastermind like himself. How wily could he be, talking that way to my best friend? I guess he figured Blackie would jump at the opportunity to dump his partner. Whatever, Blackie looked back again and I winked at him. I'd already made up my mind to rip the guy off for the drugs.

We dropped Blackie in New Jersey, where he set up distribution, and I did the same thing with contacts in the Bronx, Queens, Brooklyn, and Staten Island. Tudor had no idea how to dispose of the stuff, so we kept it at a nice duplex I'd rented on Rockville Avenue in anticipation of setting up housekeeping with Patty.

The cash started rolling in almost immediately. Tudor stopped by the duplex once a week (he'd have come every day if I'd let him) to ask how much we'd made. "Two grand," I'd tell him.

It had actually been twenty. Suspicious by nature, he insisted on taking inventory of the remaining stock. "Fine," I'd say, bring out the scales, and make the false weighing: I'd added rocks and sand to the marijuana, benzocaine and lactose to the coke. Mr. Mastermind couldn't figure it out.

Blackie and I had collected about $85,000—Tudor believed it was $30,000—before he began to wonder and grew belligerent in his questioning. The deal had about played out, so I let him have it. "Jackie," I said, "I heard every word you told Blackie on the trip up from Key West."

"What are you talking about?"

"I heard you call me a dirtbag. And white trash. I heard you say you were gonna toss me away." I'd begun to work myself into a rage.

"Frank . . . Frank . . . I'm your friend. I'd never say things like that. You must have been hallucinating."

Now I was really furious. Most of the stuff in front of him was white sand, lactose, and baby powder. I picked it up, stormed out the door, and started tossing it into the air, scattering it to the wind.

"Are you crazy?" Tudor shouted as he rushed to join me in the frontyard.

"I'll throw it all away!" I said.

Neighbors came to their windows and doors, mouths agape, watching me throw the white stuff skyward.

"Frank, come to your senses," Tudor pleaded. "Look, I'm sorry. I—"

"Get away from me!" I roared, beginning to enjoy my own act. "Don't ever come back here again! If you do, I'll kill you and your whole family!"

He left, genuinely believing I'd kill him. And I might have.

The show I put on for Tudor ranked as Little Theater compared to the dual-role Broadway-type performances required each day for Patty and Frankie. Actually, I was comfortable in both. I truly loved Patty, and felt right at home being a mob tough guy. I managed successfully to switch from one part to the other because both were genuine.

Patty planned a full-blown wedding at Olivet Presbyterian and insisted we meet beforehand with the preacher. When I made it clear I preferred a simple Justice of the Peace marriage, the minister said, "Perhaps that contributed to your first marriage ending in divorce. It's important to do this right in the eyes of God."

I halfway believed him.

★   ★   ★

Three days before the wedding, I made my weekly delivery of collections to Frankie and told him we needed to talk for a moment. I wanted to remind him that, because of my marriage, I wouldn't be around for a while.

"It can wait," said Frankie, more excited than I'd ever seen him. "I got some *great* news for you." He looked at me solemnly. "You're up."

"Up" meant I'd been scheduled to whack somebody. Afterward I'd be like family to him.

"You've waited a long time for this," Frankie said, placing his hand on my shoulder. "But the time's finally come. I know I can count on you."

My head spun as I grasped the craziness of the situation. I looked forward to wedding the woman of my dreams—in fact, Patty waited outside in my Cadillac, not knowing the purpose of my visit—and revving up for a murder didn't seem like a proper preparation for approaching the altar. I feared marrying Patty would subject her to heartache, but a killing at this time, even though she wouldn't know, struck even me as a terrible abomination, a bloody stain on our sacred union in front of family and friends.

"No, man," I said to Frankie. "I can't do it. I'm getting married in three days."

I'll never forget Frankie's look: complete puzzlement, (*nobody* had ever turned something like this down) quickly changing to rage.

"You gotta do this," he hissed.

"I can't."

"You owe me . . ."

"Not this one, Frankie. Not now."

"You better believe it's now."

"Didn't you hear me? My wedding is in three days. I'm not spoiling my wedding by whacking somebody."

Frankie tried tact, something foreign to him. The hit must have been very important. "Don't be a jerk," he reasoned. "This is your chance, don't you understand? The big guys have plans for you, and if you refuse, pal, you'll never amount to anything."

I wouldn't do it and told him so again. "Maybe later," I said. "Can't this wait?"

"No, it can't wait!" Frankie screamed at the top of his lungs. He was acting so nuts I put my hand in my jacket pocket, gripped my gun, and pushed the safety off. I started edging toward the door to get away from Frankie, reach my car, and escape from this madness. "My wedding is this weekend," I told him again, hoping somehow he'd understand.

He didn't. To him, refusing a mob order was unthinkable. "Go ahead," he raged, following me outside, "wreck your future for a bimbo. Pass on this and you'll be a brokester the rest of your life."

Patty heard the "brokester" part—I'd reached the sidewalk, moving fast for the Cadillac—and she looked alarmed at the anger in his voice. I sped off before Frankie made me suicidal enough to shut his big mouth.

"What was that about, honey?" Patty asked.

"An unhappy customer," I replied, still playing the role of successful businessman. I reached over and squeezed her hand, feeling good about myself. I didn't know how the refusal of Frankie's order would play out (refusing to obey a guy like that just wasn't done), but sitting next to Patty I had no regrets.

"Why was he so angry?" she persisted, dampening my virtuous mood.

I hated what I had to do next because it would hurt her, but this sort of interference needed to be nipped in the bud. "Just stay out of my business," I said curtly. "That's separate from you and me. I won't have no meddlin' in my business affairs."

Patty gave me the silent treatment the rest of the day, a powerful weapon, but I just had to endure it. She didn't know the source of my money, only that it was always there. The truth would not set me free; it would cost me Patty.

Responding to a musical cue, I took my position in front of candlelit bouquets decorating the altar of Olivet Presbyterian and faced the hundred guests in attendance. If ours had been a wedding at sea, a traditional bride's side/groom's side seating arrangement would have capsized the boat. Mostly the guests were Patty's family and friends; across the aisle, in attendance as my family, sat Mom and Pop Klein, plus a few of my more respectable-looking friends, sworn to be on their best behavior, including my wiseguy pal, Big Sal. I noticed, but didn't think it significant, that my buddy Jimmy wasn't present. I'd heard that he and another guy I knew had done the hit I'd turned down.

When the pipe organ began the familiar wedding march, all eyes fell on the radiant bride gliding toward me on the arm of her father—a man surely apprehensive about "giving away" his daughter to the likes of me. Still, we got hitched without a hitch, so to speak, and after the minister finished, Patty and I recited personal vows to each other. What I said to her represented more of what I should be than what I was:

My Dearest Beloved,

I pledge thee my every living breath—none shall I give my love to above thee except my God.

And may the Lord give me the strength to turn from the temptations of life that I may love thee with the purity of a Christian husband, to comfort and strengthen thee, to understand and forgive thee without question or reason.

I vow thee my love from this moment on and wed thee Beloved in this promise I make: I shall neither forsake your trust nor leave you until my death. I ask my God here and now, in His house before our families, to give us forgiveness for our past and to bless our marriage with His love and guidance through all the days of our lives.

I love you, Patricia Minucci.

Thank you, Jesus.

The parts about "God" and "Jesus" were for the benefit of Patty and her family, and as I read them now, they seem terribly hypocritical. Patty herself was a strong, quiet believer, but not a regular churchgoer. She certainly didn't wear her religion on her sleeve. As for me, thoughts of a Supreme Being had rarely crossed my mind.

Regardless, the love I expressed for Patty in that vow was 100 percent from the heart.

All of the guests adjourned to a champagne reception at the Naimo residence, and that night a limo whisked the closest family members to the Rainbow Room at Rockefeller Center for dinner and dancing.

Our honeymoon, begun a week later, differed from most in that we took Patty's father and stepmother along. It was a chance for Anthony to spend time with a daughter who lived in Miami. I grew closer to Anthony, who seemed torn between liking me and fearing I'd bring disaster to Patty. He didn't know the extent of my criminal activities, but his paternal instincts told him everything wasn't up-and-up.

Patty and I sunned ourselves on white sand beaches, visited DisneyWorld, took airboat rides through Okefenokee. I loved our week in Florida, even managed to relax and reduce the scheming about what I'd do when we set up permanent housekeeping in the duplex on Rockville Avenue.

I can't imagine a newlywed more in love than I was, yet when we returned to Staten Island, I still didn't have a clue about how to live. The way to happiness, I thought, involved making piles of money, showering my lady with gifts, and buying a dream mansion on a hill. I had several hustles in mind, but before I could launch anything new, I had to deal with the fallout from the hit I'd turned down. I learned that my friend Jimmy had been identified from the pieces of his shot and dismembered body that washed ashore on a nearby beach. His partner on the hit was shot five times, cut in half, and found rotting in two steel drums in an abandoned warehouse. In addition, Frankie and his top associate, in the cute way newspapers put it, "had disappeared."

Frankie's mom offered a $25,000 reward to anyone who found her son, dead or alive, but no one ever collected. My opinion—and it's only an opinion—is that he's either squashed in some old car or rests on the bottom of the ocean after being invited on a fishing trip.

Clearly, the guy Frankie had whacked possessed sterling connections and my former boss had gone too far. It didn't take a genius to figure out that Jimmy's fate would have been mine if I hadn't turned the job down.

Frankie's disappearance didn't sever my business ties to him. I knew I'd be expected to continue collecting money for "him" that we'd put on the street. Expected by *whom*, I didn't know.

I kept on picking up the vig and occasionally the principal and waited for the inevitable day when someone came around. Needless to say, I made absolutely sure there would be no book-keeping errors.

It took a month before two apes in suits appeared at my door. They mentioned a name in Brooklyn—a household name—and an address, and said he wanted to see me, right away, not tomor-row, with the money and the books.

I drove to Brooklyn with Big Sal, who waited in the car while I went inside. I guess I figured Big Sal could tell them what a swell guy I was if they didn't like the count. The man sitting behind a mahogany desk in his study, flanked by two large, unsmiling associates, asked, "How much you got for me?"

Without flourish, I pushed a shoe box in front of him, plus a notebook packed with code names and figures. He thumbed through the entries with the acumen of a corporate accountant, didn't bother to check the shoe box, and said, "You done good. You're responsible for the rest of the money," he added.

"Right," I replied, and he told me the name of the guy I'd deliver the cash to each week. It took two years to collect it all, but finally I succeeded.

At home on Rockville Avenue I tried, more or less unsuccess-fully, to hide my activities from Patty. I stored bundles of marijuana in a locked room, but naturally she got a look at them. This prompted a flurry of hurt questions, followed by "mind your own business" answers, then a cooling period between us I hoped never turned to a freeze. I didn't know how to handle the situation. If she'd just glance the other way, I reasoned, our marriage would be fine. *I* could lead two lives—why couldn't she?

But she loved me—looking back, it seems a miracle—and insisted she could help if only I'd confide in her. That route, I remained convinced, led to disaster. It would be like whacking myself.

I tried to buy her silence, plying her with expensive jewelry, beach and mountain vacations, flying, sailing, wining and dining in the best spots. But the attempts to corrupt her failed. When I asked, "Are you having a good time?" she'd say, "Yes, but . . ."

Patty missed having friends in the neighborhood. The neighbors, who had monitored the dope-strewing episode and black sedans and shady-looking characters at the duplex before I'd moved the family in, had gossiped to the rest until they all stayed away. Patty wanted a regular life with a husband she could be proud of and a houseful of love, but my only response to reports of snubs was, "Who needs them? We've got each other."

My in-laws visited frequently, and I had trouble fending off questions about what I did for a living. I showered Anna with presents, but Anthony Naimo knew what I was up to. "Frankie," he said, "you're gonna hurt my daughter. Don't you love her?"

He knew I did. He also knew that wasn't enough. "We're not like this," he said. "You're going to break her heart unless you change." I wanted Anthony Naimo's approval, thought of him as the father I'd never had, but deep down I couldn't accept that Patty would love me without the upscale lifestyle I provided.

The interrogation by in-laws and Patty, however gentle, began sending me into rages. A number of times I threw furniture around the duplex and threatened to leave her. On occasion I became so angry I stormed into my marijuana storage room and puffed a mega-joint to calm down. I was smoking a lot of grass and had started using speed again. The speed provided a false sense of security and courage that helped excuse my behavior.

I was dealing pot and THC, collecting vig, taking numbers, and stealing boats, this latter a profitable sideline I'd developed with Blackie. A few wiseguys checked my report cards, learned my grades had always been good, and offered me jobs with their crews. But with what had happened to Jimmy fresh in my mind, I tried to keep some distance from the mob. Also, I'd decided, working for someone else was not the route to a fortune. The trick, as successful mobsters knew, was having other people earn for you.

Other times, though, mainly to mollify Patty, I briefly tried legitimate jobs to cover my real money-makers. As a swimming pool salesman, one of the first customers I called on was thinking of replacing the pool he had. We'd barely started talking when he sniffed the cologne I wore and said, "You stink."

I must have heard him wrong. "What did you say?" I asked.

"I said 'You stink.' It's the—"

None too confident in either the social graces or sales departments, I punched the guy and threw him into his pool. Later I explained to Patty that maybe there weren't a lot of jobs for which my experience and short fuse qualified me.

A little later, in the summer of 1980, I bought a hot dog truck and began selling wieners out the back. Patty was really pleased. Profits were $200–$300 a day, which she judged plenty. The best part was I could sell hot dogs whenever I wanted, or take the day off if the spirit moved me.

One bright morning Patty and I decided to picnic at a park in New Jersey. Anthony and Anna would take Salvatore for the day, and we talked about it being "like old times."

Not far from Staten Island, in Whitehorse, New Jersey, a sheriff's deputy with time on his hands turned on his flashing blue lights and pulled us over for a cracked windshield. He seemed friendly and I figured he'd let it pass with a warning ticket. Instead, after radioing my name to headquarters, his attitude changed. He returned to the car with gun drawn, made me get out and spread my legs, patted me down, handcuffed me, stuffed me into his patrol car, and off we went.

What in the world was this? I asked questions but the suddenly grim-faced deputy wouldn't answer. It was like he'd caught Jesse James.

Patty followed us, but by the time she parked the car and got inside the station, I'd been locked in a cell deep in the bowels of the jail. Several deputies came back to stare at me, as they might a captured beast, and I could actually *feel* their hatred and hostility. I heard one of them spit out the words "cop killer."

An hour later the sheriff showed up. I learned from him that a police officer had indeed been killed, and that when my name got entered, the computer kicked out warrants tagged "armed and dangerous." The mistake the deputies made began to make sense.

"Where are the warrants from?" I asked the sheriff.

"Rahway."

"DeStefano," I said, and explained to the sheriff that those warrants were a dead issue because the statute of limitations had run out. "If you'll check, you'll see I'm telling the truth."

"Well, then, you got no worry." The cop didn't seem a hardguy. If anything, I judged him a little embarrassed by his deputies tagging me as a cop killer.

"Look," I lied, "I've been straight for a long time. I've got a wife and kid and a business in New York. The fact those warrants still appear on my record is just DeStefano's way of busting my chops."

The sheriff thought this over. "Nah," he decided. "Nobody holds a grudge that long."

"DeStefano does."

The sheriff didn't buy it, and I didn't want to dredge up too much detail to prove my point. I believed he wouldn't be so friendly if he learned about my earlier one-man-crime-wave reputation. In fact, he'd probably identify with DeStefano's point of view, that I'd never been properly punished.

"What about bail?" I asked.

"There won't be any. At least not yet."

"What are you talking about? You got me for a cracked windshield. Why are you holding me?"

"Because DeStefano asked. He's coming to get you."

I hardly recognized my old nemesis. He had to be in his mid-fifties (I remembered a more vibrant, tougher guy), and his hair had turned snow white. "I finally got you," he said, entering the cell and moving to cuff me.

"That's not necessary," the sheriff said.

"It *is* necessary," said DeStefano.

The two got into an argument, which the sheriff won because DeStefano trod on foreign turf. So the Rahway detective—he'd lost a lot of weight—waited until we stepped outside the jail building before clamping the cuffs on *tight*. Almost immediately I felt circulation being cut off from my hands.

He locked me in the Rahway jail, and Patty, bless her heart, didn't know how to handle the "there's no bail on your husband" stall. DeStefano kept me cooling my heels as long as he could, 1-½ days, before I appeared in *traffic* court and learned the one outstanding charge he could make stick: a ten-year-old ticket for owning an unregistered vehicle. The normal fine was $25; the judge nailed me for $500. Maybe he hoped I couldn't pay it.

As I exited the courthouse with Patty, a cop took me aside and said, "Detective DeStefano would appreciate if you'd stop by his office."

I took Patty with me. We sat in his office, and pointing to his head, he spoke to Patty first. "I got these white hairs because of your husband."

Then he said to me, not a trace of the macho I remembered in his voice, "So I got a little revenge." He spread his hands out, palms up. "Let's let yesterdays be bygones." His last words seemed almost a plea: "Be honest with me, do I have anything to fear?"

"Not a thing," I said. "Don't you know? I'm a good guy now."

I knew DeStefano neared retirement and didn't need problems from his past marring his golden years, when he would no longer have the police department for protection. For a long time he had truly and deeply hated me, and especially that he couldn't catch me: for ripping off houses, wreaking havoc as a biker, dealing drugs. Much of this, it must have seemed to him, I'd accomplished with a brazen, in-your-face attitude.

Studying him in his office, I realized that bone-deep he considered me a real bad guy, at least as close to one as he'd get. And, I was. At that moment, despite my anger at the $500 fine and the short imprisonment, I felt respect for DeStefano. He had tried to do his job and had earned a reputation as an honest cop (nothing to sneer at).

(Note: In 1995, we each still patronized the barber of our youth, Mike, and DeStefano learned I'd achieved slight fame in another field—he asked Mike to obtain an autographed picture for him, and I obliged.)

The hot dog business went the way of swimming pool sales. I didn't have the heart to plug away at it, nor the temperament to adapt to unexciting, everyday routines. Why, I asked myself, should I grind out a few hundred dollars through long hours of labor when thousands waited to be made in minutes?

My excuse to Patty was the nightly string of tickets (at $50 each) I garnered for parking a commercial vehicle on a residential street (in front of our house). This was hardly an insurmountable barrier, but I made it seem like a fatal blow to my hot dog business.

Except for a two-week stint at a Staten Island Pathmark supermarket, where I reunited my security crew and made the place strictly off-limits to thieves, I concentrated on selling drugs through late 1980 and into 1981. Mostly I peddled pot (I had accumulated bales of the weed in our garage and attic) and much of the duplex became closed to Patty. She continued to bear with me, hoping and praying for change, when anyone else would have given up. Even the September 3, 1980, birth of our son Angelo didn't slow my frantic wheeling-dealing. I sounded ridiculous even to myself when I told Patty it was good little Salvatore finally had a friend to play with.

As the business grew, I bought Patty more expensive jewelry and furs, and even two boats: one for tuna fishing ninety miles offshore (*I* was the tuna fisher, but the boat was "hers"), plus a cabin cruiser for family outings. Maybe, I reasoned, some quality time spent together would help.

It didn't. My efforts to buy her simply didn't work, they never worked, and the silences between us grew longer, tenser, more strained.

I hatched a plan to make so much money even I would feel secure. Then I'd get out of the rackets. I hadn't forgotten the cocaine experience with Jackie Tudor and how profitable that had been. So I reestablished contacts in Florida, confident the money I'd earn from cocaine would make my marijuana dealings seem like the mere cottage industry it was.

Chapter 11

In the summer of 1981, I became the owner of a moving business, trucks and all, through a guy in Brooklyn who couldn't pay his large cocaine debts. The man had a thriving business, a wife and kids, but snorted it all up his nose.

The moving business seemed like a perfect front to me, and I talked it up at home to Patty. But she'd seen my act too often. Still, more for show than anything else, I actually took on a few moving jobs.

More important, through the moving company guy, I had met a Colombian import-export agent who resided in the Red Hook section of Brooklyn. I'll call him Little G. He drove a BMW and Silver Cloud and lived in the kind of posh apartment that motion picture producers use to portray prosperous drug kingpins. The apartment had Asian rugs worth tens of thousands of dollars each hung on the walls, a couch too valuable to sit on because it had belonged to some French king, priceless paintings, a dozen Tiffany lamps, and a glittering chandelier imported at great cost from a castle in Europe. Little G dabbled in fencing stolen goods—furs, jewels, expensive cars—and changed Rolex watches as often as most men changed their socks. Mainly, though, he dealt in cocaine, more valuable than gold, and so pure you could step on it (dilute it) twice and still have extremely high-grade stuff.

Little G liked me, took me to parties where he introduced me to his friends, all the time observing and sizing me up. I knew he wanted tough, stand-up guys, and expected him to make a good offer—but just how good surprised me. He drove me to a waterfront mansion on Long Island and said he'd like Patty, me, Salvatore, and Angelo to live in the house—"Treat it as your own"—and *he'd pay me* $2,500 a week. The mansion, I knew, would serve as a storage depot for the large amounts of cocaine the Colombians imported. "All you do," Little G said, "is *babysit* the merchandise."

Tempting as the deal was, the part of me that treasured Patty and the boys turned it down. I couldn't put them in that much jeopardy. I knew certain things Little G and his people were notorious for, like killing entire families when something went wrong. This gang ranked much worse than the Italian mob; once you did a single job for them, they felt they owned your life and everyone in it. I'd heard about their grisly work from unimpeachable sources over the years. The Colombians didn't think twice about butchering babies, or a family dog, to make a point. I thanked Little G for the opportunity, pretending I was happy with my small corner of the world.

I used Little G as a supplier. He always had any amount of cocaine my customers ordered. I had set up my own distribution system through a half-dozen friends who started calling themselves the Sixpack, and no one got near me except these guys. They dealt with the street dealers. I was insulated from the petty hassles and petty rats who usually brought people like me down. A few times the Sixpack did moving jobs, or home repairs (through another company established as a front) to establish legitimacy to our lives. Most of the 1981 summer I spent lolling with my family on one of our boats.

On New Year's Eve, 1981, I drove to Little G's apartment in Brooklyn and found a party in progress. Little G invited me in. Present were several businessmen, doctors, lawyers, accountants, even a police official. Their bond with Little G: All used thousands of dollars of cocaine a week. They were valued customers.

I sat at a long polished table with the others drinking champagne and sampling hors d'oeuvres. Soon Little G brought out the pièce de résistance, a silver tray on which sat a silver spoon and a half ounce of cocaine. The doctor on my right cut a line, snorted, and handed the tray to me. I passed it along to a Japanese businessman saying, "I don't do this shit."

Soon the tray came around again. The doctor cut a line and said to me, "You needn't worry. This drug isn't addictive, you know."

"You're crazy," I said. I had a moving business that proved it is.

"Maybe psychologically it is," the doctor said. "But physically, no. What cocaine does is enhance the user's self-esteem. And his performance." He snorted the powder and said, "Try it. You'll like it."

I took the tray and started to hand it to the Japanese, but the doctor touched my arm. "Surely trying it once won't hurt. I'm a surgeon. I know. Use it once and I guarantee you'll be thanking me."

I looked foolish, felt like a flat tire at that table, slowing down everyone's good time. People stared at me; even Little G watched with a wondering half-smile on his lips. I cut two lines and snorted them.

It was the worst move I ever made in my life.

The reaction came instantaneously. I looked down my nose at the surgeon and thought, *This guy ain't nothin'. I'm a hundred times smarter than this sawbones will ever be.*

I felt my mind had been flushed clean, as if for the first time all the rubbish hindering and clogging my brilliant thought processes had suddenly been expelled. I found myself to be a master conversationalist, a fountain of new ideas, witty, charming, and sophisticated . . . I was a genius, the best and the brightest.

Basically, I'd always been insecure around people, especially educated ones, but cocaine elevated me to an intellectual plane superior to everybody. I discussed market trends with a stockbroker; corporate bankruptcy tactics with a lawyer; and the trade imbalance with the Japanese. I snorted a mind-enhancing white powder line every time the tray lapped the table, and I didn't drive ("fly" would be a better word) home until 8 A.M. New Year's Day.

Today, when middle-age sometimes jades my understanding of how peer pressure negatively influences young people, the only wakeup call I need is remembering my follow-the-crowd behavior at Little G's. More than any guest present, I should have known to say "No" to this incredibly dangerous drug.

Treacherous and devious, coke never lets the user know what's happening until it's too late, and maybe not even then. Since the individual experiences no immediate or debilitating side effects (quite the opposite, in fact), his brain absorbs the wrong message: The drug is *good.* Cokeheads invariably fall in love with their "new and improved" selves.

As I was about to learn, this is the bottom line on cocaine: It launches deadly attacks on the lungs, liver, kidneys, and brain, all the time convincing the user that it's good for him.

For me, there was no tentative dipping of toes into water to test the temperature. As a dealer, I had mounds of cocaine and no compunctions about using them. The white powder made me feel on top of everything.

Recently we'd moved to a large single-family home with a cathedral ceiling in the upscale Bay Terrace section of Staten Island, a place with a great deal more space between neighbors and additional room, I thought, to conceal drugs from Patty. The place featured a big backyard and a view of the water. We could walk to our boats. More important, with a big assist from the coke, I felt like a drug kingpin, greeting and issuing orders to my trusted Sixpack.

Soon I learned about free-basing. A friend saying "You ain't seen a real high yet" came to the house with vials, medicine droppers, ether, various solutions, and a bong pipe. He mixed the coke with other ingredients, shook them into a milky white solution, and allowed them to settle until a cotton like substance formed in the bottom of the vial. On top of the substance stood a crystal clear solution, ether, which contained 100% pure cocaine. My friend, using a medicine dropper, drew the clear liquid from the vial and squirted it onto an object resembling a large contact lens. I watched with fascination as the ether evaporated and snowy flakes formed. With a razor he scraped the flakes into the bong, then heated the bowl of the pipe.

"Suck the vapor out," he instructed. "Hold it in your lungs as long as you can."

The result: the "best" high I've ever had. Instant and extreme. I became euphoric, floating naked on soft clouds in a utopia I never wanted to leave. If I wasn't already addicted, I was then.

I didn't know that the first high from free-basing is the most intense an individual will ever achieve. He'll chase and chase and never catch it again. I've known people who smoked cocaine and threw away fortunes, chasing that first high until their hearts exploded.

My life became a merry-go-round of selling and free-basing, but it wasn't enough just to kill myself. I needed company. Ominously, responding to urging from me (as I'd responded to the doctor's), the Sixpack started using and soon were addicted.

I couldn't ingest enough of the stuff. I snorted and free-based what seemed mountains of the junk and soon my thoughts were spaced and I found myself forgetful of duties and deals. I grew paranoid and slept with an M16 rifle and hand grenade at my bedside. I never left home without at least two guns and secreted other guns throughout the dwelling for easy access. Our once-beautiful house in Bay Terrace was transformed into a fortress with a dizzying array of locks and deadbolts on every door. Nights became days, days nights, and I seldom saw my family. I was awake while they slept, and vice versa. My life was falling apart.

In mid-1982, I still had money and connections, but was func-tioning very poorly. Mostly I lurked behind locked, solid doors, smoking cocaine to the tune of $750 a day, and dealing only with the Sixpack, whose own performance had fallen off markedly. I allowed them to extend credit to unreliable street dealers and generally stayed too wasted to keep abreast of the day-to-day functioning of business. At first I had felt safe in my house, but soon security could only be achieved in my own bedroom. I was a sick animal crawling deeper inside himself.

Street dealers began ripping off the Sixpack. No surprise there. Street dealers always try to rip off suppliers—a disciplined crew is needed to keep them in line. But we couldn't keep anybody in line, especially ourselves. Achieving the almost impossible, I began operating a thriving cocaine business that managed to lose money.

Besides the paranoia, a coke addict can count on becoming extremely selfish. He reaches the point of not sharing with anyone.

Everything is me, me, me. The smallest transaction is based on what it does for *me*. In the past, whatever my motives, I'd been generous with gifts and loans. No more. Minucci the Miser, Scrooge reborn, appeared on the scene, grilling Patty about even routine household purchases.

Of course, Mr. Cheapskate was also Mr. Jealous. I accused Patty of sneaking out for trysts with boyfriends. Once I snatched the phone from her hand, certain I'd caught her talking with a lover, and found myself on the line with Anthony Naimo. I shouted at him, accused him of urging his daughter to leave me. This turned out to be true enough. He'd have been less than a caring father if he'd counseled anything else.

I started ripping off regular customers by authorizing the Six-pack to sell them oft-stepped-upon coke. Soon people who had trusted me were threatening my life because I'd cheated them so badly, and I escalated the rhetoric by saying I'd kill them *and* their families if they didn't quit complaining.

For a long time I imagined myself an all-powerful drug lord, but in reality I'd become a cocaine-crazed fiend totally out of touch with the real world. Patty's family stayed away and she and the kids were terrified of the monster in the bedroom.

One night, early in 1983, I sat tensed on my bed, thinking about a meet I had with Little G. I played it over and over in my head, becoming convinced he would rip me off, and planned how I'd handle the inevitable shootout. Just then I saw movement out of the corner of my eye—out of character, I'd forgotten to lock the bedroom door—and knew for sure Little G had come to kill me in my own house. I dove on the figure in the dark and jammed my gun into his face, a microsecond from squeezing the trigger.

"Dad!" a voice cried out. "Dad! It's me, Ronnie!"

I'd almost killed my oldest son, age nineteen, who had come to live with Patty and me because, I contended, my income would provide him with a "better life."

When I met with Little G, I learned he had no intention of killing me. He had something else in mind. "Frankie," he said, "we've had a good run together. But I can't sell you no more coke."

The saying "No one so blind as he who refuses to see" applied to me. I actually asked Little G, "Why? Why are you cutting me off?"

"Think about it, Frankie," he said, not unkindly. "I hope you straighten yourself out."

"I haven't cheated you," I said. There were other suppliers who clamored for payment, but Little G I'd wisely kept up-to-date.

"I know, Frankie," he said. "And I don't want it ever to come to that."

Who needed him, I thought. I was a major druglord in my own right and didn't need these murderous Colombians. There were plenty of other sources of supply, and sure enough, I found them.

Trouble was, I started ripping *them* off. I took coke on consignment, the Sixpack distributed it to street dealers on consignment, and all those consignments coupled with theft and our own prodigious usage meant I couldn't pay the new suppliers. No problem, I figured. I'd simply find new sources of supply.

Patty was at her wits' end about me. She wanted out of the marriage, "Not because I don't love you, but because you won't change. The truth is, Frank, you've gotten much worse."

She said she couldn't stand watching me kill myself. That's how she talked. Not a word about the pain she suffered. I snapped at her constantly, called her filthy names, threatened her father and stepmother, and several times was physically abusive.

My behavior with the children (besides Salvatore and Angelo, at one time or another all four of my other children came to live in this "better environment") was verbally abusive in the extreme.

If I'd retained a shred of decency, I'd have noticed the horrible physical and mental toll I was taking on my beautiful Patty. But, as I've pointed out, a full-blown cokehead acknowledges only his own needs.

The nonsense stories I gave suppliers became more far out. The idea was to get the cocaine fronted so I could cut it, grab a share for myself, sell the rest, and put away the money from that. When the coke was gone, I pulled the same scam again, and once

I'd run through all the dealers, I returned to the first one with the money I owed and a made-up tale of why it took so long.

Almost all my time was spent in a twilight fantasy world locked in my bedroom, unable to and uninterested in keeping track of who owed whom. Large debts built between me and my suppliers, thanks in good measure to the Sixpack owing money to me because of street dealers ripping them off. I added Blackie Zeal to my inner circle, but he succumbed to the same easy money temptations we had. Soon Blackie owed me $22,000 for coke I fronted him, started making excuses, and finally stopped coming around at all. Blackie, I'm sure, never used the junk; his problems, like ours, were street dealers he'd foolishly trusted.

The main problem was me. If I had run a tight ship, there would have been plenty for all of us. By becoming my own best customer, I lost control of how the business got run.

It wasn't long before a supplier stuck a gun in my face, and another threatened to rig my car with a bomb. Patty and the kids used that car, and the threat temporarily enervated the Frank Minucci of biker days. Along with two coked-up members of the Sixpack, I went to the supplier's house late one night while he was away, robbed it, and trashed it: a loud and clear message to stay away from my family. This guy had connections, but I'd grown so insane I didn't care. There were times when death seemed welcome. The robbery and trashing took place in November 1983, and when I survived until Christmas, I wondered if it were some warped present from the Grim Reaper.

Early in 1984 Anthony came to the house for a face-to-face. It took courage on his part because he knew I'd become nothing short of a murderous-minded maniac. Well, not one hundred percent, because a tiny slice of humanity remained that reminded me how much I admired and loved him. He stood in front of me and called me an "evil drug addict fiend" who had never loved his daughter.

My brain spun as I listened to his righteous abuse, but I never made a move toward him. I wanted to shut his mouth, stop the truth that gushed from it, but something held me back.

A few days later, after I'd locked myself in the bedroom, Patty took Salvatore and Angelo and moved to her parents' home. She left a note saying she loved me but couldn't stay unless I sought serious help and made drastic changes in my life. I read the note again and again, devastated, gripped by fear that turned to sorrow, and for the first time since childhood I felt tears running down my face.

I had really lost Patty.

But maybe not forever, I consoled myself. "Seek help," she'd said.

I didn't want help. Help meant no more cocaine, a condition my brain said I couldn't endure. The junk was fast killing me, but I'd die anyway at the hands of one or another enemy, and the agony of trying to get better would have been for naught. Coked-up, my death would be painless. At least that's what the drug said, and it said more: *I'm your only friend. I'm always here and I don't judge you. Who else provides comfort?*

On the other end of the tug-of-war rope pulled Patty. *Painless death?* I imagined her saying. *Look at yourself now. How can the suffering be worse?* Back and forth it went, Demon Drug versus Loving Wife, all played out in my mind in the big empty house. I decided I had to coax Patty back. The cocaine? I'd buy myself some time. Who knew what might happen?

I dragged myself to a medical doctor (Patty would want proof of my good intentions). I told the doctor about my roaring coke addiction and he wrote out a prescription for Valium. The result was I ended up with another drug problem, the last thing I needed.

Patty came back, grasping for straws. I made promises I couldn't keep but she wanted to believe them. Despite all evidence, that rare love she had persuaded her of what *might* be: a potential for good no one else recognized, including myself.

Also, things had been hard for Patty during her short stay with Anthony and Anna. They had asked questions but she couldn't confide in them. The whole stinking mess racked her with shame and despair. And what could she say when, disbelievingly, they heard she was coming back? How about this: "Oh, this was only a temporary setback. As soon as Frank gets through his gangster/drug addict/raving lunatic phase, everything will be peachy."

Of course she couldn't say that. She came back to Bay Terrace over the most strenuous and loving objections.

Things got worse. The Valium knocked me down, so I free-based more cocaine to climb back up. I needed to deal with the scummiest lowlifes just to maintain the coke supply at a trickle.

I was totally wasted, a walking corpse in search of a grave. I couldn't form a rational thought or utter a sensible sentence, and my body functions began to fail: I passed blood in my urine and stool, my lungs congested, my nose was raw and ruined, and my remaining teeth started rotting out of my head.

Somehow I continued to exist, though I could barely walk. I stumbled from room to room, chair to chair, my vision blurred. The one function I could perform was ingesting more cocaine.

I became a complete recluse from the world and my family, seldom lurching out when anyone was awake. Patty communicated with notes slipped under the door. One read, "I'll always love you. I wish you'd let me help." Another said, "Remember the quiet town in New Hampshire? Wouldn't it be nice to go back?" A third urged, "Maybe if you pray to God, He will help you."

I crumpled the notes and threw them away. At times, in a trance, I imagined myself happy. No one could hurt me here. Formless images flickered in my head and were gone.

The few times late at night that I embarked on zombielike staggers through the house, the rooms seemed like foreign places, strange chambers I'd never visited before. I thought my senses were keener than ever, able to detect different aromas in each room, the slightest variations in temperature, and subtle changes of light and shadow. Actually, I existed in a netherworld, all alone and truly insane.

One morning before dawn Patty found me stone-faced in the kitchen staring at a wall. "Frank," she said softly, "can you hear me?"

I could hear her, all right, but I grunted something incomprehensible.

"Sweetheart, would you like to talk?" she said. "I'll put on a pot of coffee. We can watch the sunrise."

A black bile boiled in my brain. "I don't need coffee," I growled. "I don't need you."

Her sweet smile faded. She put her head in her hands.

"Don't think I don't know," I said hatefully, "about your sneaking around behind my back."

But she didn't leave.

September 1984 dragged into October and still I didn't die. I hardly ate; my stomach wouldn't hold anything as sensible as food. Much of the time I had no idea if I was alive or dead. The only true thought I had—and this time it *was* true, I knew with absolute certainty—was that I had reached the final few closing days.

Chapter 12

On cold, damp November 1, 1984, my aching bones and troubled body that hadn't enjoyed a restful sleep in months lay across the bed listening to a country singer on the radio blaming the world and some woman for his problems. Country music enriched my feelings of self-pity, and besides mumbling nonsense conversations with myself, following woeful tales of cheating hearts, phantom truckers, midnight trains, and prison blues helped pass the time. Working up a thirst during another tear jerker, I got up in search of water and, with confusion overriding paranoia, forgot to lock the door behind me.

When I returned, Angelo sat on the bed fiddling with the radio dials. Angelo, age four, looked like a short inverted curly mop, and had enough curiosity to shame a cat. His eyes bugged out when he saw me in the doorway, and he scurried from the off-limits territory.

Angelo had changed stations on the radio before turning it completely off, so when I pressed the Power button, I was listening to a talk show. I reached to turn on the country station, but the word "cocaine" coming out of the speaker assured my attention for a few more seconds.

Some guy was telling about how cocaine had done a number on his life. He'd lost his wife because of drugs, his childhood sweetheart, and very nearly blew his high-profile, high-paying job.

"Here comes the bull," I mumbled to myself, and sure enough he started talking about religion: Jesus this and Jesus that. Jesus helped him change. Jesus helped him. Jesus saved his life.

Too lethargic to move my fingers, I listened but figured his testimonial had no meaning for me. Jesus, God, devils, and angels . . . that stuff was looney tunes. Money and cocaine were my gods, and Jesus a crutch for weak people. I'd had a few run-ins with religion as a boy in various foster homes—Sunday School and such—and what good had it done for me? Patty, and the pastor who married us at Olivet Presbyterian, had talked about God, but I was a hard case who didn't need help.

The man on the radio started to sob. Normally I despised crybabies, but for some reason I kept listening. I learned the speaker's name was Darrell Porter, a baseball player, recently the most valuable player in the World Series. Realizing the guy wasn't a wimp, I tried to pay closer attention.

Porter said God had worked a miracle on his life, given how low he had sunk. He'd betrayed everyone—his mother and father, his wife, his teammates, his friends—in his mad craving for cocaine. Now he had me hooked. I had the eerie feeling he was in my room talking directly to me. I experienced disappointment and emptiness when the show went off the air.

Even though Porter temporarily hooked me, I quickly wriggled free. I went back to my country music, and thirty minutes later had my nose in cocaine.

Two days after I felt like a visitor at my own death watch. I'd been snorting cocaine like crazy (it required too much energy and concentration to free-base) and swallowing Valium to level off. I was oblivious to everything around me. My brain pounded a pain worse than any I'd ever known, and I feared my skull would explode.

The agony carried into the early hours of November 4. My eyes were puffed nearly closed, and several times I thought I'd pass out. I tried doing lines of coke, but they made me feel faint and nauseated: chasing the high had finally led to no high at all.

My left arm and fingertips tingled, and flames shooting through my chest felt so hot I believed a heart attack was near.

At 3:30 A.M., barely able to walk, I went to where Patty slept and laid next to her. Trembling uncontrollably, I thought, *Here you are, Mr. Tough Guy, moaning and dying like a craven coward.* That's what I thought of myself: a spineless punk, physically wrecked, mentally shattered, scared and helpless and waiting to die.

The crushing, smothering chest pains combined with the thunderous roar in my head made it impossible to lie still. I lurched from the bed, chasing a breath, then one more, and staggered on weak legs from room to room, my body now *freezing,* moaning in utter misery. I was barely aware of Patty behind me, saying words I couldn't understand.

Even with blurred vision, I could make out the mound of coke on a large mirror drawing me like a magnet toward the dining room table.

It'll make you feel better, my mind advised.

I took a nosedive, plunging my face in the cocaine, like that famous scene in *Scarface,* and felt flash-frozen: my nose, lungs, and throat turned instantly to ice.

"Please, baby," I heard Patty say, "let me call 911 and get you some help." Braced against the table, I felt her wrap a blanket over my shoulders.

"Don't call nobody," I mumbled, and pushed away from the table.

The room spun wildly, but much worse than that, my entire body was freezing from within by blood that had turned to ice scraping like tiny glaciers through my veins. The chilling frostbite numbness seized my extremities—fingers, toes, penis—and I wet myself. Then, in the torso, it locked down my lungs; I gasped and gasped but there was no air.

Collapsing on a chair, I started choking on my tongue. I few moments later, Patty tells me, I went into convulsions. I heaved violently for maybe twenty seconds and finally was still.

The next thing *I* knew I was falling, like you do in a dream, falling but never hitting bottom. I sped through a long dark tunnel, spinning as I went, picking up velocity, headed down and down.

A million . . . no, an *infinitesimal* number of thoughts vied for my attention, but overpowering them all was the most profound feeling of sadness. I knew I was leaving my beloved Patty and my children behind.

As I plunged down the tunnel, I glimpsed a white light in the distance, and a feeling of warmth and well-being replacing my icy desperation. I heard a voice—Darrell Porter's voice!—saying "Jesus, Jesus, Jesus," and my mind's eye pictured Patty, doubled over, tears streaming down her face.

I knew I was dead, or dying, and I screamed as I plunged, "God, please! If You are real, don't let me die like this. I promise, I'll change my life."

Suddenly I stood in front of a figure dressed in white robes. I couldn't see his face—the light was too bright—but I noticed a golden rope around his waist and a pair of golden sandals.

I wasn't afraid. Quite the opposite. And just as the ice had fanned through my veins, now something warm began to fill me. With the warmth came a deep sense of peace and gentleness.

A voice emanating from the flowing figure said: "It is not your time. Go back and tell them of me."

An instant later—not even that long—I was back on the dining room chair, my head resting on the table. A smell of flowers filled the room. My throat and lungs felt warm again, no longer frozen, and a gentle thawing heat traveled the length of my body, like an internal defrost spreading from top to bottom.

The most amazing feeling—utterly unforgettable—was the sense of being healed. As the warmth enveloped me, I could feel my body gain strength.

Better yet, Patty could *see* it. She stared at me, wide-eyed, wearing a smile of puzzlement and wonder. Right in front of her I seemed to grow younger. "How do you feel?" she said, a hopeful light in her eyes I hadn't witnessed for a long time. When I didn't answer, because I had no reply, she said, "Go look at yourself in the bathroom mirror."

I did. Walking on sturdy legs that burst with power, I went and viewed a reflection that could have been the framed picture of a stranger. I blinked and peered again at the *radiant* countenance, one worn by a father holding his newborn, or a child on Christmas morning. I marveled at the metamorphosis. I seemed new—brand new.

"What in the world happened?" I wondered aloud. "Was I dead? Did I really see *Christ?*"

I stared again into the mirror. Absolutely no sign remained of the horrific cocaine addiction that minutes earlier had collapsed me like a damp rag. It was as though a master plastic surgeon had removed the lines and sags and made my face smooth and healthy again. But the difference was apparent in much more than my face. Every nerve and sense, my entire body, seemed reborn.

"Tell me what happened," Patty said. She stood behind me rubbing my shoulders.

"You tell *me,*" I answered. "Did I die on that chair? What did *you* see?"

"Sweetheart, you weren't breathing. I held you and cried and prayed. A minute went by, no more than that, and then you opened your eyes."

"It seemed longer than a minute."

"I don't think so," she said. "Then when you woke up . . . came back . . . your face started to change. It was like a magic slate, starting at the top, but it erased only the bad things."

We went into the dining room, sat among the white powder, which seemed no more than a messy inconvenience (it held no appeal for me), and I slowly and carefully recalled for her what had happened. I remembered every detail. I still do.

"Tell me again," Patty said, "exactly what Christ told you. It *was* Christ, you know that, I hope."

"He said, 'It is not your time. Go back and tell them of me.' "

"Christ wants you to do good work. He brought you back to life so you could."

I nodded, hoping my story would be happily ever after from now on but, though physically rejuvenated, I had a long road to travel on the spiritual front. Even as Patty spoke, a heavy chill crept over me, dark and evil: my past calling me to the future. Not even a half-hour had elapsed since a miracle brought me back to life, and already I felt myself succumbing to temptation.

I looked at the mound of coke in front of me, my mind racing, and suddenly felt overwhelmed by all the unfinished business that lay ahead. I wouldn't be spreading anyone's word unless I took care of it quickly.

Patty read my thoughts and knew exactly what tore at me. "I guess all this can go now," she said, waving her hand at the white powder, her voice both a plea and a demand.

"I need to think!" I snapped. Already I sensed danger closing in. The debts I owed, the deadly, unforgiving enemies I'd made—neither would go away. "I don't know what's going to happen," I said to Patty. "I do know I've got business on the street."

"How can you say that?" she cried. "God just performed a miracle in your life. "He . . ." she continued, but she was talking to an empty chair.

I stomped to my former bedroom prison, locked the door, and sat in near-despair on the rumpled, sour, sweat-stained sheets. It broke my heart that I'd made Patty cry, just when it seemed we had hope, but what hope did we really have? I thought of all the people I'd cheated on drug deals—the worst crowd on earth to cheat on anything—and believed the extra life I'd been granted would soon be forfeit. I thought of Christ again and wondered if all of it had been a joke. Had I been spared death by drug overdose to die by gunfire, or maybe much worse?

Dread of what lay ahead clashed with the recent, crystal-clear memory of my encounter with the man in white at the end of that tunnel. Recalling the peace and goodness that permeated my every fiber, I couldn't believe a prank had been played on me, or that I'd imagined the entire episode. I did look and feel different, and the maniac craving for cocaine had vanished. Still . . .

St. Thomas owned no advantage over me in the doubting department. Why would Christ save me, my mind nagged, to be gunned down by drug dealers?

I went to the closet, pulled down Patty's large family Bible, held it in my hands, and turned my eyes to the ceiling. "God, is this your word?" I asked. "That's what I've heard. I'm told you speak to people through the Bible. Well, I'm going to look in your book."

Was I really going to threaten God? I hoped He wouldn't view it that way, but I really didn't know any other way to phrase it: "I promised to change and I will," I said, "but if this book doesn't tell me that what happened was You, then both of us have wasted our time."

The words were barely out of my mouth when a soft, full voice surrounded and engulfed me: "My son," the voice said, "Ezekiel 37: 5 and 6."

As I'd later preach in hundreds of churches, and myriad other places, I knew plenty of Vinnies, Tonys, and Vitos, but not a single Ezekiel. What happened next, since I know about odds, seemed still another miracle. I opened the Bible directly to Ezekiel 37 and the words seemed to jump off the page at me: "This is what the sovereign Lord says to these bones: I will make breath enter you, and you will come to life. I will attach tendons upon you and make flesh come upon you and cover you with skin; I will put breath in you and you will come to life. Then you will know that I am the Lord."

I dropped to my knees, weeping like a baby, and gave very belated thanks to God for giving me back my life. Once again I experienced the warmth banishing the chill I had felt beginning to return when I'd been assailed by worry. The bedroom seemed filled with light, gentle against my tear-filled eyes. I *knew* God was real, and that he had saved me and had a plan for me. I remembered again that I'd made a promise to change, and on my knees in the bedroom I vowed once more that I would.

Light of step, feeling twenty years old, I walked out to Patty and held her in my arms. "We'll make it," I said. "We'll be all right."

"I love you, Frankie."

"And I love you."

Over the next week, along with the physical healing, came a healing of mind and heart. I discovered a much greater depth to my emotions, and a conscience, hitherto muted and deadened, that allowed me to bear witness to the evil my life had represented. I intended to atone for that evil and started by amazing Salvatore and Angelo with a newfound awareness of their feelings and needs. After the initial shock, they began to like their new dad.

Over that first week I also buried myself in the Bible, a starving man ravenously consuming every morsel. Clearly my entire existence had been an abomination, yet there were messages of forgiveness even for such as me. Especially in Biblical proverbs did I find blueprints for a new life.

Early on I shared my near-death experience with everyone I could find to listen. Mostly I got greeted by skepticism—"What scam is he up to now?"—but not from Patty, the kids, Patty's family, or even the Sixpack. All these *saw* the difference in my appearance and attitude. My face and body had overnight shed ten years, and I moved with a briskness of step that had been physically impossible a few days before. Anthony and Anna Naimo took one look, then gave me marvelous hugs. Perhaps everything would turn out okay.

I had much to do and very little time. It seemed a hundred pressing issues needed to be resolved. How could I make a living? In what way could I best serve God? And always, how do I stay alive long enough to do it? God helps him who helps himself, I believe, but I had problems knowing how to start with those murderous characters who wanted me dead.

On November 11, 1984, I received a phone call from Don Swantek, a friend from Jersey I hadn't seen in eighteen years. "How ya doin', Frankie?" he asked.

"I'm doin' great," I said, which was only part true. I could feel the past catching up with me.

Swantek and I had been close through our teen years, and through word-of-mouth I knew a little about his life. Just five-three and light as a feather, he possessed a fine voice for rhythm and blues (fans said he sounded like Ray Charles), and had carved out a successful career for himself as the opening act for some of the most famous names in entertainment, including the Four Seasons and Neil Diamond. He had cut his own record and seemed headed for bigger things, but booze and drugs caught up with him first. A terrible car accident nearly killed him, but luckily, it caused him to examine his life and ultimately led him to God. When he phoned, having heard of my near-death experience, I knew he'd become a well-known and much-sought-after evangelist.

"I heard a miracle happened to you," he said.

"Yes." I told him what happened.

He started to pray for me over the phone. The words sounded strange coming from him. I remembered a little guy with a cocky attitude and permanent chip on the shoulder, hustling/shuffling his way to the top of the byzantine world of rock. Full of jive and not much substance. I agreed, with reluctance, to allow him to come to the house and pray with me.

I knew I'd experienced a profound religious experience, but it hadn't wiped from my mind—it never would—a deep cynicism about the motives of individuals. What I'd seen, the way I'd lived, made me suspicious of people, particularly of "holy ones" who seemed to make a lot of money "ministering" to others. I hadn't seen anywhere in the Bible, and I was reading it a second time, that Christ had urged his disciples to live fat off the land. To the contrary, his own life argued against the accumulation of material goods.

Don Swantek looked natty in expensive jeans and a silk shirt, which set alarm bells ringing in my head. I noticed he took good care of his hair because the few he had left were combed carefully in place. I watched him like I would a poisonous snake, but couldn't find a trace of the phony in my old friend. That first day, and all the days that followed, right to the present, he showed complete dedication to God. No tricks. No faking. No hustles.

We prayed together for two weeks, Patty often joining in, and he helped me interpret the Bible. A good and patient teacher, he had insights into what the Good Book said that I never could have gleaned on my own.

I confided to Don the *sine qua non* of my staying alive: paying off my debts to the mob and other suppliers even more ruthless. One of these, a guy with no bull in him, had called to announce my whole family would die if I didn't soon come through with his cash. I told Don my chances of survival would be better racing through hell in gasoline-soaked drawers than ignoring warnings such as this.

"You need to ask God what to do," Don said. "You better than almost everyone knows that God answers prayers. I promise, there's a solution, and He'll help you find it."

Late that night, praying and reading the Bible, I came to the part where the rich man goes to Jesus and says (I'll paraphrase in the language of the street), "I want to follow you, Jesus. You know, join your gang. Become one of your boys."

Jesus answered, "Sell all you have, give it to the poor, and follow me."

The rich guy shook his head. He couldn't do it.

Christ said, "It's easier for a camel to pass through the eye of a needle than for a rich man to enter the kingdom of heaven."

The story flipped me out. Here was a guy standing right next to Jesus, in Jesus' time, knowing Jesus' miracles, and he blew his chance to be with him. I knew precisely what that scripture was saying to me.

I called to Patty and asked her to join me in the dining room. She had been studying the Bible as closely as I had, and she'd fallen deeply in love with Christ; after all, Christ's intervention ended my drug use and had begun to make a difference in me as a person.

"I'd like you to read this," I said, and pointed to the story of the rich man.

When she'd finished, I said, "I need to pay off these debts, baby. It's the only way out. We need to sell everything we have."

This kind of "giving away" riches may not have been exactly what God had in mind, but it might accomplish both goals: rid ourselves of unneeded possessions, and keep me alive to do God's will.

Patty smiled and without a word headed for the bedroom. She returned, carrying every piece of jewelry I'd bought her over the years, plus a pair of fur coats I considered special because they'd been anniversary gifts. She laid everything in front of me and said, "Whatever it takes, as long as it gets you out for good."

I looked at her, tears welling in my eyes.

"I love you, Frankie," she said. Even in the worst times she had never stopped.

Everything I'd ever bought her—gold, diamonds, valuable watches—sat in that pile. She'd even added her engagement and wedding rings from her first marriage.

I sold almost everything we had, including the boats and moving trucks, much of it at a tiny fraction of its real value. In a desperate hurry, dickering over price seemed wrong.

My first stop was a Brooklyn social club. The wiseguys playing cards and drinking coffee did a double take when they saw me. "You finally snort one line too many, Frankie," one of them said, "coming here like this?"

I said, "You should know God so loved the world that He gave His only begotten son, so whoever believes in Him shall not perish but have everlasting life."

"Hey, Frankie's seen the light! Praise the Lord!" a wiseguy named Vinnie guffawed. Everyone laughed, but not in any manner meant to make me feel secure.

I smiled, shrugged, and headed for the man behind the big table, knowing all the religion in the world wouldn't help if I didn't take care of business. I dropped a brown paper bag on the table, along with an up-to-date tally book. He studied the entries, like most bosses a whiz at arithmetic, then emptied the bag in front of him. It contained more than I owed. He counted out his share— I wouldn't have argued if he'd taken it all—and handed the rest back to me.

"Hey, Frankie," he said as I turned to leave. "How long you figure you'll last till you're back?"

"I ain't comin' back."

"What you gonna do?"

"I'm thinkin' of helpin' kids who are hooked on drugs." The words just came out, but it didn't seem a bad idea.

"Yeah, sure." The boss laughed. Everyone in the room was cracking up. When I'd almost reached the door, the boss said, "You'll be back."

"With God's help, I won't be." I knew the words sounded strange and phony, but they came naturally to me. Still, I remembered how I'd reacted in the past when I met someone claiming to be born again, and understood where their heads were.

And why not? These guys knew me. They had worked with me. Oddly, the boss had it right. I would be back, though not for any reason he imagined.

I took a deep breath outside the door of the social club. The dreaded encounter had gone far smoother than I'd expected; thanks, I believed, to God, who knew nothing calms an angry creditor like being paid. Standing there, I remembered the faces, and believed I'd seen traces of uncertainty, several tough guys with hurt in their eyes, wondering if maybe what they witnessed had been genuine: that I'd found freedom while they remained trapped in a savage dog-eat-dog netherworld.

I'd been a "hopeless" case. Down the road, sometime in the future, I vowed to find out if *they* could be helped. That would really be something.

High on joy, I sang, laughed, cried, and praised the name of Christ on the drive home. I picked up Don Swantek. He'd said he wanted to accompany me, stand by my side, share the danger like a good Christian brother should, and I'd agreed, provided things went okay on that first stop.

Don and I spent the rest of the day, and several more, calling on a varied group of drug suppliers, paying what I owed (more than $35,000), and moving on. I enjoyed watching the absolute surprise on their faces. Never dreaming they'd see their money, they had expected to collect in flesh.

I paid all my debts, plus those of the Sixpack and Blackie Zeal. My friends had been deathly afraid, but when they thanked me, I said, "God paid what you owed."

I took to family life as though it was what I'd craved all my life. The kids loved their new father, someone who had time for them, and Patty said I'd become the caring husband she'd always known had existed under the brutal exterior. Whenever someone asked what had precipitated the change, I told the truth: Christ had saved my life, brought me back from the damned, and I owed Him everything.

I studied the Bible—alone or with Patty and Don Swantek— every free moment, taking a crash course on God's words. Especially the passages on redemption and salvation filled me with wonder. They opened a whole marvelous world I hadn't known existed.

I wish I could report that I metamorphosed from evil to pure good, but nothing of the sort happened. Despite vast improvement in the quality of my life, I wasn't close to a 180-degree turnaround. No money came in to support my family, and several times, when an old customer called, I hooked him up with a new dealer, pocketing money for the referral. Rationalizing I didn't actually sell the stuff, I nonetheless couldn't con my conscience and always, in the aftermath, prayed feverishly for forgiveness.

Unable to maintain the hypocrisy, I told Don Swantek what I did, and he went nuts on me. "That's the devil, man," he raved, "trying to make you fall out of God's grace. Don't do it anymore. Not ever."

Don cooled off and explained that I needed to eliminate everything having to do with my dark past—friends, hangouts, *possessions*.

"Give me a break, man," I said. "That's everything in this house. Even that little rug you're standing on."

I got no sympathy from this guy. "I'm telling you, you need to dispose of anything you'd be ashamed of God seeing if He visited your home."

I wrestled with the problem late into the night. Every way I looked at it, Don was right. My possessions had already largely disappeared, paying the drug debts, but I realized they *all* had to go. I wondered if Patty and the children would empathize when they found themselves sleeping on the floor.

At 3 A.M. I opened the front door, turned on every light in the house, and began throwing our possessions into the frontyard. I worked like a man whose house was afire, lifting, humping, dumping, racing inside for more. Patty, Salvatore, and Angelo soon woke up, sat on the living room couch (till *it* had to go), and watched what seemed like a madman at work.

It took more than an hour to throw everything out (later I called a Goodwill Industries truck to carry it away) and then I slumped on the floor, exhausted and soaked with sweat.

"Sweetheart," Patty asked, "what was that all about?"

"We just got rid of the last of the devil's possessions," I answered. "We're free, Patty; we are finally free."

I went to the pantry and took out the olive oil and went from room to room, chasing away the evil that once had roamed there. I made the Sign of the Cross in oil over each room, then prayed over my family—I believed I was clean, forgiven, and sealed in the hand of God.

Chapter 13

We moved in early 1985 from the big house in Bay Terrace to a comfortable but far less imposing duplex on Ada Drive (where we still live) in Staten Island near the Gothels Bridge that leads to New Jersey. The first floor has a living room, large dining room, kitchen, and bathroom; upstairs are three bedrooms, another bath, and a rather unusual view from the second-story deck: the Baronhurst cemetery. We thought the quiet neighborhood of middle-class families would be a good place to start over. Patty was ready to put down roots, make some real friends, and share a normal home life with her "changed" husband. Normal's what I wanted too.

Patty's sister Frances and her husband Patrick helped us obtain furnishings, and Patty found work in a clothing store. I obtained a regular job at a meat company owned by Peter Castellano, Jr., the nephew of organized crime boss Paul Castellano, known as "The Pope," who in a few months would be gunned down in front of Sparks Steakhouse in Manhattan.

The job was strictly legitimate. Peter Castellano, a Christian businessman, had heard through the grapevine about my religious experience, and readily hired me when I asked for work. He had a history of helping poor people and others who needed a hand. The job entailed a lot of lifting, throwing heavy slabs of meat around: excellent training, the foreman assured, for managing a retail meat market operation.

Don Swantek introduced me to Pastor Paul McCarthy of the nondemoninational Evangelistic Center in Rahway, and McCarthy invited my family to join his congregation. After a long talk with him, we accepted. McCarthy struck Patty and me as deeply religious, sincere, knowledgeable about scripture, a true disciple of the Good Shepherd, dedicated to gathering stray sheep into the Lord's fold. Combined with my intensive home Bible study, he'd help me, I was sure, learn more about Christ.

I attended regular Sunday services, heartened by the congregation's acceptance of me. But I didn't deserve it. People called me "Brother Frank" (the name stuck), but I felt like a hypocrite because I still hadn't cut all material ties with the past.

One Saturday in March, carrying a cardboard box, I called on Pastor McCarthy. I'd flushed every ounce of cocaine down the toilet when I disposed of my possessions; but I'd kept something even more valuable. In the quiet of McCarthy's home, I showed him the contents of the box: hundreds of blank birth and baptismal certificates worth, conservatively, $1.4 million. By filling in the blanks, residents of Latin American countries could be turned into Puerto Ricans, and therefore citizens of the United States. I'd held back these certificates, as insurance, while throwing out everything else. Now I handed them over to Pastor McCarthy and suggested he burn them.

"I've got a better idea," he said.

The next morning, during services, he guided the congregation through a history of my life (prior to this, they'd known only bits and pieces), including my near-death experience, and ending with the delivery of the birth and baptismal certificates to him. "Brother Frank wants them destroyed!" he cried, and dramatically, the worshippers transfixed, he shredded $1.4 million in documents in front of them all.

During Sunday services Pastor McCarthy occasionally performed healings. A lifelong cynic, I watched him like a hawk, but never detected even a trace of hanky-panky. A woman, confined to a wheelchair, got up and walked. A year later she was still walking. An arthritis victim, after being prayed over, was suddenly free of pain. Pastor McCarthy never took credit for the healing. Christ did the work, he averred. What could I say to that? Christ had cured *me* of a terminal cocaine addiction. He'd done what medical science couldn't.

"Anyone," Pastor McCarthy told me, "can serve as a conduit for God's healing. By faith, a true believer becomes an open channel through which God's power flows and restores health to the afflicted."

Not me, I thought. But God had another surprise in store. The first of many healings—miracles, really—I participated in started in modest fashion. Angelo had an inner ear infection, and a visit to Doctors Hospital on Richmond Road brought assurances that a prescription would clear things right up. But the medicine didn't help. A refill did no better. Angelo lay crying on the couch for three days.

A retired cop, Jim Howard, a member of Calvary Assemblies of God church, paid a neighborly visit and tried to comfort Angelo. "Have you prayed with him?" Howard asked.

"I've said prayers every night."

"Did you lay hands on him?"

"No, I haven't."

"You should give it a try. It might make the difference. Let's pray with him together."

Why not? We went to Angelo, and Jim put one hand on his forehead, the other on his ear, and prayed. "Heavenly Father, we lift this child up to you right now. We call upon the written word of God. For it is written that by His stripes we are healed. I curse this infection at its roots. I call out the pain in the name of Jesus. So let it be done as it is written. Child, be healed in the name of Jesus!"

The healing was instantaneous. I saw the burden of pain lift from my son's face, vanish in an eyeblink. "How do you feel, Angelo?" Jim Howard asked.

"I feel good," he said. "Daddy, my ear doesn't hurt anymore. How did he make it stop?"

"It wasn't me, son," Jim answered. "It was the healing hand of God."

Ten minutes later Angelo was outside with friends, riding his little bike.

My second brush with healing occurred at Pastor Raymond Eppolito's Victory Fellowship Church in Clifton, New Jersey, where I'd been invited in September 1985. As I launched into the usual recount of my notorious past, which would climax of course with my near-death experience, I found my eyes drawn to a seventy-year-old man who had been introduced to me before the service. A powerful attraction pulled me toward him, and leaving the lectern, I walked over and stood in front of him. I put a hand on each ear and for a split second sensed confusion raging in his head. Colors flashed before my eyes, and I heard *his* mind thinking, "I can hear."

I told his daughter, who sat next to him, "Take your father to the back of the church. Talk to him in a normal voice. Please, just do what I ask."

"I can hear!" he shouted before his daughter could move from the pew.

Those words are etched in my brain—"I can hear!"—and also the joy and wonderment I felt when he shouted them. Best of all, he still hears today. Praise the Lord.

I'll recount just a few more experiences I had with healing—there were many—but want to emphasize, as Pastor McCarthy did, that they were strictly the work of God answering prayers. I had *no* power of my own; humility and gratitude were the emotions I felt when someone was made well.

One day I went to Staten Island's Westshore Auto Sales to do my favorite thing, talk up God to someone who'd listen: this time, reluctant Westshore owner Harry Shaughnessy and a young guy from the neighborhood named Richie Frontero.

As we talked and Harry smoked a big cigar on the sidewalk in front of the car lot, a couple walked toward us. Suddenly the male pedestrian moaned, doubled over, and collapsed to the ground. The woman bent down, touched the motionless figure, and wailed, "Help me!"

Just then a St. Vincent's Hospital ambulance drove by. The

driver sized up the situation, hit the brakes, and backed up. Two paramedics scuttled out the back door and rushed to the fallen victim. I walked over, followed by Shaughnessy and Frontero, to watch. The paramedics started trying to shock the man's stopped heart back to life.

"Why don't *you* try to help him, hotshot?" the irreverent Shaughnessy breathed through his cigar.

Exactly what I'd been thinking. I muscled between the paramedics, put my hands on the exposed chest, and said: "I rebuke the spirit of death in the name of Jesus! Release this person now! I speak life into him for the glory of God who I serve!"

The man got up.

"What the . . ." Shaughnessy said, the cigar falling out of his mouth.

The paramedics, glancing leerily at me, assisted the victim into the ambulance where he collapsed again. They tended to him frantically, furiously, and one of them said, "I'm getting a flat line."

"Didn't work for long, I guess," said Shaughnessy. If it had been a few thousand years ago, this Irishman would have cheered for the lions.

I ran to the ambulance and grabbed the man's feet. "Satan, release him now in the name of Jesus! Spirit of Death, I rebuke you! In the name of Jesus, release this man now!"

He sat straight up and the startled paramedics laid him back down. "Who are you?" one of them asked.

"A servant of God." I crawled into the ambulance and looked into the man's eyes. "Give thanks to Jesus," I said.

The next day he was released from St. Vincent's Hospital, with no symptoms of the attack that had stopped his heart. Shaughnessy thought I had used some "trick" to shock him back to life, now he believed. Richie Frontero, more openly impressed, took me aside. "Frank, my mother is scheduled for a hysterectomy and she's very frightened. You think God could do something for her?"

"We'll find out," I said, and prayed with Richie. When his mother entered the hospital a few days later, the doctor couldn't medically explain what he found: it turned out she didn't need an operation.

Richie Frontero became a devout believer, especially after I convinced him it hadn't been me. A few weeks after the incident with the heart attack victim, he visited our home and confided that his wife couldn't have children. "Will you pray with me on that?" he asked.

We did.

Today they have two children.

Blackie Zeal and I resumed our friendship (I went back too far with him to sever all ties), and came to me worried about his daughter, Dawn. She had a cyst the size and shape of half-a-banana on her left leg. The doctors were talking serious operation, and Blackie wondered if I could help.

I knew Dawn—she'd been there as a little girl when her parents cold-turkeyed me off speed—and loved her like I would a daughter. What if my prayers fail? I wondered. I went to Pastor Paul McCarthy, confided my concerns, and asked, "What if it doesn't succeed?"

The usually soft-spoken, mild-mannered McCarthy got hot. He shook his head and scolded, "Your doubt is what will keep the prayers from being answered." He made me kneel in front of the cross and pray with him.

The next day Patty and I called on Dawn in her Jersey home. "Do you believe in God?" I asked her.

"Yes."

"Do you believe God can heal you?"

"Yes."

"Do you believe Christ is the Son of God?"

"Yes."

I placed my hand on her cyst and prayed. The evil growth collapsed under my touch.

Pastor McCarthy urged me to become a preacher. "You have a unique testimonial to give," he said. "There are many sad and lost souls wandering hopelessly that only a gifted person like yourself can reach. God has blessed you, Frank. You should think about putting His power to work through a ministry."

"Aren't I a little old for that?"

"Christ didn't think so when he spared your life. He told you, didn't he, to spread his word. What better way than this?"

Me an ordained preacher? It seemed preposterous. I told Patty what Pastor McCarthy advised, and we prayed long and hard seeking guidance. Gradually we began to believe the idea wasn't so crazy: some of Christ's best disciples had been anything but Boy Scouts.

I had just quit my job at the meat company a week earlier. A lot of rough guys worked for Peter Castellano, Jr., and though some of them didn't object to my frequent talk about salvation, others did, and complained to a foreman. He came to me and said, "You want to be a meat manager or a religious nut?"

"Religious," I said.

"Well, you can't be. Not on this job."

So I quit. Peter Castellano gave me a week's severance pay. Had I asked, this believer in Christ would have put me back to work, but God had other plans for me.

Pastor McCarthy's Evangelistic Center carried satellite television college classes from a Texas-based bible college. I threw myself into the study of advanced Bible courses. Nights, as a family, we read scripture and discussed what we had learned.

For the first few weeks, I reveled in the televised courses. The Bible, the greatest of all books, contained so much wisdom I couldn't have begun to absorb, understand, or interpret without expert guidance. I scribbled copious notes, went over them each night with Patty, and rejoiced believing I'd at last found my calling.

In a few short weeks, though, my perspective changed. The instructors from the college started focusing less on the Bible and God's Word and more on how to raise money for the church. It was always "the church," and how funds were needed to keep it strong.

"If you give your best," an instructor told us, *"you'll* be well taken care of."

Another said, "God wants his ministers to become rich."

I couldn't find that anywhere in the Bible, nor could I locate the give-give-give message we were urged to browbeat the congregation with. The poor sharing their much-needed welfare checks with the ministry represented an investment God would return to them manyfold, according to the TV instructors.

A few times I suggested a clothing drive for the poor, or a food distribution center, but the answer always came back the same: "God will help these people; we don't make allocations."

Soon I was taking a faith-healing course and being told about the "healing explosion" currently "sweeping the country." The more I watched and listened, the more ludicrous it became. One of the most popular ailments to "heal" turned out to be tennis elbow, an inconvenience experienced mainly by affluent country club members. Very little got mentioned about healing through Christ: in fact, what they taught were *medical techniques* which often brought temporary relief, but nothing that lasted.

Wanting out of this scam, more hypocritical than any I'd engaged in on the street (when I beat a guy nearly to death, there was no pretending it helped him), I nonetheless hesitated for fear of offending Pastor McCarthy. I would meet many devout and dedicated ministers who simply couldn't accept that the motives of others were less pure.

What finally shoved me over the edge was a visit (supposedly quite an honor) from a Texas instructor who said, "You're a natural. You've got a great story to tell. Your testimony will draw people in droves."

The guy came armed with a contract that stated all monies I raised had to be turned over to the church. "Don't worry," he said slyly, "God will take care of your personal needs."

"I don't want anything to do with your outfit," I told the college's emissary. "Take your contract and get out. You've seen the last of me. I don't steal from God."

He looked genuinely puzzled. I turned on "The Stare"—every mobster, even a retired one, has it—and he beat what he hoped was a dignified retreat, fortunate he hadn't met me several years before.

The dream of becoming a minister had been planted, however, and with Patty's help we paid tuition to continue my studies through the Billy Graham School of Evangelism, a correspondence college I can recommend unreservedly. The lessons consisted of no-nonsense audiotapes which I listened to with Patty again and again. There was none of the grab-the-bucks hype.

No play and all work, even if you love the work, can sap even the most energetic individual. Besides carrying a full-time college load, I helped with the bills by painting churches, the homes of churchpeople, mowing lawns, driving a taxi—I even took a newspaper route delivering *The New York Times*. Often when things became hard, loved ones from the church would help us with food, money, love, and prayers. One family, the Romeos, practically adopted us. They are genuine people of God, and we owe them a lot of thanks for the unconditional love they showed us over the years. It was through Ralph Romeo that I learned never to count what you give in the name of God. If you can help, then help, joyously, and let others see Christ in you. It does wonders for the heart.

One day in the duplex, my brother-in-law Patrick and I were talking and the TV happened to be tuned to a bass-fishing program. "There's a sport you'd enjoy," Patrick said.

"Nah," I said, but started to watch.

"You need a pastime. You haven't got any life at all except religion."

"That's enough." But the anglers, no pun intended, had started to hook me. Earlier I'd enjoyed fishing for tuna, but clearly this took more skill. I decided to give it a try and have never been sorry.

In fact, I gave it more than a try, first taking Patty to streams in New Jersey, then entering largemouth-bass-fishing tournaments. To jump ahead a moment, in 1991 and 1992 I won Master Angler awards from *In Fisherman* magazine; an Angler award from the North American Fishing Club in 1992; and another award in 1993 from the Red Man Tobacco Company.

In October 1985, I received a phone call from Pastor Carlos Garcia of the Love Chapel in the Greenpoint section of Brooklyn. Of course, like everyone in the New York religious community, I knew about and admired Pastor Garcia's work. His large church (capacity 1,200), housed in a former theater, ministered to the poor and disadvantaged.

"I've heard positive things about you," Garcia said. I frequently delivered church testimonials, by invitation, and assumed he'd gotten wind of one of those.

"I'm honored you'd call," I said.

"We've got to meet," Garcia said. "God woke me out of a sound sleep last night and told me to help you in any way I could. The doors of my church are open to you. Can you stop by for a talk?"

I went the next day and stayed a year and a half. Pastor Garcia, a Puerto Rican in his early fifties, was stocky and just five-feet-seven, but towered like a giant to everyone who knew him. It filled me with pride that he'd asked me to join his church. The Love Chapel clothed people, fed them (who can listen to accounts of God's love when they're hungry?), and housed the homeless. More like an actual father than a pastor, he accepted a very small salary from the church and restored furniture during his infrequent spare hours to make ends meet. High among his good works were a day care center he operated free-of-charge for welfare mothers and a center for troubled and battered women. Patty became involved with this center; she took courses to learn counseling methods, and plunged wholeheartedly into the work. It's not an exaggeration to say she was a natural. Just as important, she felt as obligated to God as I did—she couldn't forget that the Lord had given her husband back.

Name an urban area of need, and Pastor Garcia addressed it. He persuaded public school teachers to tutor dropouts, operated a class that taught illiterates to read, and made sure addicts found the help they needed.

"I've got big plans for you," Garcia told me. "I want you to be a full-time volunteer."

"I'd like to be a minister."

"And so you shall."

I'd obtained credits from the classes taken through Billy Graham, and by correspondence courses through the Pentecostal Holiness Bible School in North Carolina. I thanked him and enrolled in another fine institution.

As promised, Garcia took me under his wing, allowing me to participate in all the church programs. I even spent time tending toddlers in day care, but was more effective counseling drug abusers and arranging for them to get help.

Pastor Garcia liked my sincerity and dedication. Patty and I purchased sixty minutes a week on WWDJ-AM, 95.7 radio, and we cohosted a call-in program between 9 and 10 P.M. on Fridays. The program—*Turn On to Jesus*—attracted a large, dedicated audience.

Our program consisted of a twenty-minute inspirational message letting people know God had not forgotten them, no matter how bad things seemed. Then we took phone calls from persons who wanted prayer and counseling on a wide variety of problems. During our "Love Thy Neighbor" segment, our operators took calls from people who needed clothes, blankets, furniture, food, even a car, and matched them to callers who were blessed to donate the items needed by the less fortunate. "Any of you good folks out there," I'd say, "who can use some food help, don't hesitate to call. Ain't nothing wrong with needing a hand. God loves you, and so do we."

Not surprisingly, the switchboard stayed jammed all the time we were on the air. Church volunteers stood by to pick up donations and deliver to those in need. It wasn't for lack of interest or listeners that the program was lost. The station raised the price of air time and we couldn't afford to continue. We discussed seeking donations to maintain the broadcast, but feared becoming trapped in a fund-raising quicksand. While it lasted, though, *Turn On to Jesus* provided needed assistance when none was available elsewhere.

Patty and I developed an alternative that Pastor Garcia endorsed. We established a 24-hour phone line—718-494-PRAY—that people could call to make donations that we then distributed. This line is still in operation.

My experience with the greed of that Texas-based TV ministry made me leery of charlatans, and I took time whenever I could to check them out. A well-known preacher from Oklahoma appeared at Calvary Tabernacle in Elizabeth, New Jersey, and I decided to give him a look.

Three hundred people came to see his amazing show. It started with him talking to an empty chair.

"God," he said to the chair, "it's great to have you here tonight." He seemed to listen for a moment, then moved closer. "Are you sure I should tell them *that?*" he asked in a whisper loud enough to be heard.

Still nearer he moved to the chair, listening, occasionally saying "Yes" or "Okay" or "Are you sure it's time for that?" His facial expressions were remarkable. "That's good news!" he'd exclaim. "Yes, yes, they'll love hearing that."

His object, of course, was keeping us on the edges of our chairs until he shared the "good news." Not knowing whether to laugh or break that chair over his head, I decided to pray for him. "Give me just a few minutes more," he said, "then I'll let you know what God has said."

He continued to talk to the chair.

I looked around. Some people were making jokes, others seemed to believe God was really sitting there talking with the preacher. I remembered his claiming to have spoken to Christ on numerous occasions, but I felt I shouldn't mock him. Who was I to judge whom God would and would not visit? But I did not feel God in that room, nor did any of those I talked with later that night.

How is one to know when a preacher is genuine? Pray, first of all, and trust in God. But also, look to those who do the work of Christ—feeding and clothing the poor, for example—and not to the ones who seem most interested in raising money.

During this most fruitful period with Pastor Garcia, I became much in demand as a speaker in New York, New Jersey, and Connecticut churches. My message—"You're Somebody Because God Loves You"—had a universal appeal, I think, because of its simple truth: You don't have to be rich, famous, or glamorous to rank as important in God's eyes. My story, relating the depths to which I had sunk, pounded home the point.

I also found popularity with FGBMFI (Full Gospel Business-men's Fellowship International) as a speaker at meetings, luncheons, and dinners. I gave testimony 125 times in 1½ years at their gatherings.

In November 1986, two years after the near-death experience and after completion of extensive accredited Bible study, plus thousands of hours of hands-on work, Pastor Garcia (with the approval of the Love Chapel's board of directors) ordained me Reverend Frank Minucci. At the same time, Patty was ordained as a missionary.

The "Reverend" part felt uncomfortable. I urged everyone to call me Brother Frank.

The time arrived, in early 1987, when we felt we should strike out on our own. With Pastor Garcia's blessing, Patty and I formed ChristWay Evangelistic Ministries. Patty's duties included writing and editing a twelve-page bimonthly newsletter, the idea being to reach hurting souls, as I once had been.

Chapter 14

The ministry encompassed four stages, at times each one overlapping the other three. First, the title "itinerant preacher" applied to me. Answering calls from pastors to speak at their churches, I delivered sermons and gave testimonials in Michigan, Alabama, Mississippi, Florida, Texas, North and South Carolina, Louisiana, Georgia, and Tennessee.

Patty, Salvatore, and Angelo often went with me. We drove to most of these engagements, staying in the homes of congregation members or at inexpensive motels. Our only remuneration was "love offerings," donated after the regular collection, and these were mostly churches with very poor members. Usually we lost money. For five years, 1987–91, I averaged 12 out-of-town testimonies a month, a total of about 720.

Often, while Patty drove, I wrote sermons, more than forty in all. My "I Also Have a Dream" (about the need for denominations to spend more time saving souls and less in bickering over obscure dogma) was popular at the many black churches where I spoke, while "Sir, We Would See Jesus" (in ourselves and our actions if we truly accepted the Lord) touched any congregation.

I never thought the day would come when Patty was the one concerned about finances, but as treasurer of ChristWay Evangelistic Ministries, that was her job. "Honey," she said, in the spring of 1988, during one of our whirlwind journeys from engagement to engagement, "we just can't keep this up. Every time we go on the road, we come back poorer than when we left."

"I'll have to push the audiotapes harder," I said.

"You won't do that. You know you won't."

We'd made several tapes, hoping sales would defray expenses, but usually wound up giving them away rather than accepting money from people who had very little. Patty couldn't gripe too much about this. She didn't like taking money for God's work, either.

The situation was uncomfortable for all concerned. Southern pastors wanted me to speak—they loved the message and the crowds (which meant needed donations) I drew—but couldn't afford more than the "love offerings." The extra money I brought in helped keep the church doors open a little longer.

The big churches, on the other hand, that were part of the TV faith movements, never called on us because we preached messages that underplayed giving and highlighted the message of Christ.

The few large churches we appeared at collected baskets and baskets of money, telling the people it was a love offering for us, but we received only a tiny fraction at the end of the evening. One church, we learned, took in several thousand dollars, and gave us $150. Many times I was tempted to backslide to the old Minucci and take care of a few of these con artists. Patty always kept me from blowing. She said God would deal with these pastors, and maybe he did: a few years later, three of them who had short-changed us fell from grace and lost their ministries. Regardless, I began staying closer to home, concentrating on needs in our own backyard. Maybe that's what God had wanted all along.

The second phase of our work through ChristWay involved a prison ministry. It started when officials at Rahway Psychiatric Prison invited me to speak to a group of inmates; afterward, a doctor said he had never witnessed anything comparable to the response I drew. Forty-two hardtimers, mostly murderers and all of them sex offenders, showed up to listen, and within five minutes thirty-six of them were on their knees in front of a cross praying for salvation and forgiveness.

I really got into it. After telling them briefly about myself, I launched into the message. "Man may not forgive you but Christ will. Christ can identify more with you than the noncriminal people who put you here. He knows what you're suffering—he suffered much worse—and *he* didn't deserve it. How well does Christ know you? He was busted by the cops of his time, betrayed by a rat who was supposed to be his friend, slandered by false witnesses, tried as a criminal, convicted as a criminal, sentenced as a criminal, and hung up to die between two criminals. He didn't deserve any of this, yet he suffered everything you guys have, and more. Here's someone you can turn to, who will understand your cries for help."

Word of my success at Rahway prompted officials at the Clinton (NJ) Women's Correctional Facility to issue a speaking invitation. More than anything, these women inmates needed a strong dose of self-esteem, and the "You're Somebody Because God Loves You" theme proved ideal. Prison authorities, at the urging of the inmates, invited me back.

I spoke at Sing Sing, Rahway State Prison, the Arthur Kill Correctional Facility in Staten Island, and Rikers Island in Queens, New York. Because I could talk to inmates on their level, they responded. "Your only hope is Christ," I told them, and many vowed to change.

Hundreds of prisoners reached out through the mail. Men like David Berkowitz, the infamous Son of Sam, asked me to pray with him at Sullivan Correctional Facility, and several times I did over the phone. I can't reveal what Berkowitz told me, but can vouch that his finding God is genuine. If that surprises anyone, it shouldn't.

Christ never shunned anyone, and I—a former criminal—certainly couldn't. Anthony "Gaspipe" Gasso, an alleged mob capo turned to me for help and we prayed together. He asked for forgiveness and I believe he received it.

Steve Spinelli, a convicted mob hitter, said he wanted me to minister to him. As we prayed together, he seemed to accept—especially after hearing my experience—that the message of Christ's crucifixion meant *anyone* who found faith could be saved.

"Could you do me a few favors?" Steve asked.

"Depends on what they are," I said.

"I've got two sisters. Because we're related—there's no other reason, Frank, I swear—they're having trouble finding jobs."

It was something I could handle. I went to one of my FGBMF acquaintances and found them work. In the process, I learned it was also important to attend to an inmate's more worldly concerns. The fact that he'd been removed from circulation usually extended the punishment to innocent loved ones. Each year, around Christmas, I host parties and solicit gifts for the children of parents serving time in jail, and others from poor families, and still do.

Gene Gotti, brother of convicted mob boss John Gotti, asked me to visit and pray with him. This I did, and also with the wife and family of murdered mob boss Paul Castellano.

News of my work spread and led to a pair of remarkable conversions. I can't say they really surprised me. I thought pain had been evident in the eyes of a couple wiseguys that day the drug debt got repaid, and sure enough a pair of phone calls came. Each guy spoke furtively, as though J. Edgar Hoover himself or the ghost of Lucky Luciano might be listening, but it became clear they wanted to talk about Christ. During several meetings conducted so clandestinely the CIA would have been jealous, these mob hard guys promised to "ease out" of criminal activities and dedicate their lives to the Lord. We knew it would be tricky, but through various subterfuges they succeeded.

Charles Colson, the Watergate figure, heard about my work and invited me to appear on his radio program. He had formed a large prison ministry called Prison Fellowship Ministries, so I gladly accepted. During the broadcast hosted by Ron Jacobs of the Ministries, we received a tremendous response from call-in listeners.

A short while after that program, I appeared on the "700 Club" with Pat Robertson. During the phone-in portion of the show, an unprecedented situation involving one of the callers occurred.

"I've got a gun in my hand," said the man on the phone. "I want to talk to Brother Frank before I pull the trigger."

"Let me talk to him," I whispered to Robertson.

The TV evangelist nodded and pointed to a room backstage. As Robertson assured the audience the caller would be attended to, I hurried off-camera to speak with him in private. The guy was despondent over a year-long unsuccessful job search. He was, he said, without money and without hope.

I talked with him carefully, encouragingly, for twenty minutes, about Christ, but also about finding him work. "I *absolutely* guarantee you'll find a job," I said, and he promised to cool it a few days.

"Nobody's gonna hire me, though," he concluded.

"Ye of little faith," I said, but he didn't understand the reference.

It didn't take a few days. Robertson's Christian Broadcast Network hired him immediately for a custodian position.

Christmas was the busiest time of the year for Patty and me, attending to the needs of the families of prisoners, but also reaching out to the community at large. We loved the work, plus the knowledge that we honored my promise to Christ—it was reward enough. Still I couldn't help feeling good when an article appeared in the *Staten Island Advance* written by Paul M. McPolin:

He has a red suit, rosy cheeks, a bulbous nose, a jolly paunch, a hearty laugh and eyes that sparkle behind real bificals. He also has three bullet wounds, a biker jacket, Mafia friends, hellish nightmares and a rap sheet from here to the North Pole.

His name is Frank Minucci, a.k.a. Santa Claus.

Minucci, 48, of Graniteville, is an ex-Hell's Angel [sic], ex-mob enforcer, ex-drug dealer, ex-cocaine addict, ex-husband, born-again Christian, TV evangelist, pastor, family man, drug counselor and social worker.

Watching him at the L&M Discount Variety Store at the Big Apple Bazaar, preaching love and self-respect to a child on his knee, is bearing witness to a Christian miracle. . . .

The third hat I wore with ChristWay Ministries, along with itinerant evangelical and prison minister, was in many ways the most satisfying: street preacher. Whenever possible, often four or five nights a week, I hit the pavement looking for hungry people (they weren't hard to find) and those in need of clothing and shelter. It seemed to me the work was precisely what God commanded.

I specialized in finding help for addicts, a problem with which I had a world of personal experience. Often ChristWay received calls from worried family members, the drug abusers themselves, or ministers. The pastor of a Baptist church in the Bronx, for example, called one evening to tell us about a man sleeping in a cardboard box not far from his house of worship. The pastor had fed the person several times but nothing seemed to help. Not wanting to summon the police, he asked, "What do you suggest?"

"We'll be right out," I said.

The man turned out to be Haitian, jobless, separated from his wife and family by his addiction, and pretty much, till now, without hope. Failing to find an immediate opening in a rehab facility, Patty and I brought him home, where he stayed with us three days until a bed became available at Christian Outreach in Brooklyn, New York. We regularly took in such boarders, and never regretted it. We saw the Haitian two months later at Christian Outreach, a new man, clean and on the road to recovery. The next time we met him he was working and back with his wife and family.

At Christian Outreach, I had the pleasure of working with Jimmy Pinto, one of the planet's unsung but truly great heroes. Jimmy had been a heroin addict for *33 years*. With God's help, he straightened his life out, worked through the ranks, and became an evangelist for the organization with its vast international reach.

How vast? Christian Outreach put my testimony on audiotape and distributed it at their facilities in fifty-seven countries. I'm the one speaking when the language is English, but Patty and I find more pleasure listening to the words coming from others in different tongues.

Norman Vincent Peale heard the audiotape and called it "one of the most powerful ever made."

"You're bringing us plenty of people," Jimmy Pinto said one evening. "Even without your help, you know, we'd be plenty busy."

"Yeah?" I said. I didn't get it.

"You're doing the easy part," he said. "How about rolling your sleeves up and really helping?"

That's when I assumed the duties of a Christian drug abuse counselor. Pinto was right. The hard job—isn't it always so—required firmness and love and so much more over a long period of time.

My late-night forays in search of lost souls took me to some of the most dangerous places in the local area: Fulton Street in Bedford-Stuyvesant; MLK Boulevard in Newark; 111th Street in Spanish Harlem; and Jersey Street in Staten Island. Having belonged to some tough gangs myself, I felt comfortable talking with modern versions of the old me. I told gang members who questioned my qualifications (translation: "Who are you, old man, to preach to us?") to "shut up and listen." I usually added, "I'm a little short of a Harvard degree, but I got an advanced degree from the Holy Ghost."

They didn't know what that meant, but my size and businesslike demeanor generally assured their attention.

Some of these kids I interested in God; others I couldn't reach. It never helped to speak of Christ in a milk-and-honey fashion with gangs. Of course, no need existed to portray him that way. He would have been right at home with these outcasts.

Besides the ChristWay Ministries phone number, Patty and I found another way to obtain food and clothing for the needy. Channels 24 in New York and 32 and 35 in New Jersey offer free cable television time. We took advantage of it to launch a program called "His Answer for You." Borrowing from our former radio show, we had a segment called "Love Thy Neighbor," in which viewers phoned in donations to be distributed by our street ministry. Driving through neighborhoods late at night, seeing abundant pain and anger, it troubled us that there were so few fingers in the leaky dike of desperate need.

Our own financial boat seemed about to sink. Paying for food, rent, utilities, and other necessities involved a desperate scramble each month, and the inevitable time arrived when we just couldn't make it on my odd jobs and the money Patty pulled in from the clothing store. I had to find steady employment.

Answering an ad for a chauffeur, I found myself in Manhattan talking to attorney Peter DeBlasio, age sixty, five-feet-five, a stocky Brooklyn-born ball of energy who'd been an Assistant U.S. Attorney before founding what became one of the most successful personal damage practices in the country.

I got a look at the office when I applied for the job: it occupied the entire forty-third floor of the Woolworth Building across from the mayor's office at Broadway and Park Place. DeBlasio was no ambulance-chaser in search of whiplash injuries. Airplane crashes were more his speed, plus medical and legal malpractice and products liability.

I watched DeBlasio light an expensive cigar, his shrewd eyes taking me in. *No way is he gonna hire me,* I thought. The résumé looked okay for the last five years, but before that, forget it. As we talked, I seemed to have developed a case of amnesia about everything preceding November 4, 1984. Vague responses and "I don't recall exactly" answers, however, seemed to amuse him. My voice and body language told this former federal prosecutor all he needed to know, and he didn't care about my past.

"I can tell you're okay," he said, laughing. He hired me at the starting rate for chauffeurs, and later raised the figure to almost double.

DeBlasio and I became good friends. He reminded me of Perry Mason, *if* Mason had practiced in the civil law area. Working with his world-class team of investigators, he was a whiz at establishing blame. Listening to him recreate an accident beat eyewitnessing it yourself.

Much of my job involved waiting for DeBlasio to come out of his office. With plenty of time to kill, I studied the Bible and kept an eye cocked for people to help. I had started carrying extra shoes, pants, and coats in the car, so if a guy hobbled by with plastic bags on his feet, or shivering in rags, there would be something I could help him with. DeBlasio, of course, noticed the extra clothing I carried in the car, and a few times caught me passing it out. He always acted amused.

Outwardly DeBlasio acted as if I were half-mad, but inside I think he enjoyed watching the strange bird he had hired as a chauffeur. He helped me obtain a credit card, something I believed would never be possible, and it proved invaluable when we ran out of money short-term.

Unable to carry food while I waited for DeBlasio, I struck a deal with City Pizzeria and Restaurant to serve generous five-dollar meals to anyone presenting an initialed ChristWay Evangelistic

Ministries card. I paid up at the end of each week and collected the cards to hand out again.

During the holidays, Patty and I went store-to-store soliciting donations of food, clothes, and toys. I made a point of stopping at mob social clubs and endured the usual trash talk. "What dirtbag am I adopting today?" a wiseguy could be counted on to ask. "Why can't them bums get jobs?" another would complain, and there were plenty of racial remarks.

I smiled, listened, and often walked away with more aid than Christian businessmen offered. The wiseguys viewed themselves as hard cases with a heart and were especially vulnerable to pleas for children.

Peter Castellano, Jr., was particularly generous during the holidays. He sold ChristWay and other ministries truckloads of turkeys for a few cents a pound.

I tried not to neglect my four children from the marriage with Mary. They had suffered deep scars having me as a father, but time and the Lord had started the healing process. I managed to bring them all into churches, and I pray we will all be forgiven in the end. All four are grown and married and have their own lives to look after—we exchange cards on holidays and every once in a while there's an "I love you."

In 1990–91 I entered the fourth phase of my ministerial life by renting a hall in Kenilworth, New Jersey, with another minister named Ralph Romeo, Jr., and founding the Church of ChristWay. It seemed a culmination of sorts, a dream come true, pastoring my own church, which started with twelve members and soon grew to forty-five. The church took more time than I'd anticipated and I had to quit my job with DeBlasio, who remains my good friend.

I found the new work difficult and requiring skills not so important on the streets or in prisons. I was no longer just a preacher or angel of mercy, but father figure, marriage advisor, and shrink. Members came to me with tough questions, which I did my best to answer in a Christian way, but these were the problems of ordinary people—my forte was the *extra*ordinary. In retrospect, I lacked the background and patience all great small church pastors must have and quickly gained respect for those pastors.

Also, each of us bears our own cross, and often our loads seem heavier than they are. "Don't worry about the small things," I like to say, but small things appear major to some of God's children. The ultimate truth is I was not reverent enough nor was I disciplined enough. I was rough around the edges and knew it, and my work with the Church of ChristWay became a trying experience I endured for a year and a half.

Not thinking anyone would miss me when I stepped down, I was in for a pleasant surprise. Every member of the congregation signed a petition asking me to stay. I got on my knees and prayed hard over the decision, but the answer came back the same: Not just me, but the church members, would be better served with a new pastor. My own effectiveness lay in the unorthodox approaches of the past.

The congregation gave me a going-away dinner. I thanked them, misty-eyed, for the time we'd shared. In my heart, though, I knew Christ preferred me in my other three roles rather than as regular head of a flock.

Chapter 15

William Deerfield, coauthor of *Snap Me Perfect,* Darrell Porter's autobiography, did a feature story about me and my conversion for *Guideposts* magazine. During the course of interviews, Deerfield autographed a copy of the Porter book: "To My Brother in Christ, Frank—one of the toughest 'lambs' ever to be reclaimed by the Good Shepherd."

I mention Deerfield because he served as the initial catalyst for a new and thoroughly unanticipated phase of my life. Early in 1992, while riding on a train, Deerfield met Al Levin, a HBO producer working on a TV special called *Mob Stories.* One thing led to another. Levin contacted me, and I agreed to appear on the program. He interviewed me at length about how and why I had left the mob.

After the program aired, there were invitations to appear on *Montel Williams, Joan Rivers, Sonya Live* and CNN. I loved Joan Rivers. She listened to my stories about the street and prison ministries and wrote a generous personal check. Sonya Friedman was something else. I had barely settled on a chair when she asked, "How many people have you killed?"

The only reason I'd come on this show was to talk about the ministries, and here she wanted me to rat myself out. I answered, not too coolly, "That's a stupid question." It was an unChristianlike reply. I quickly added, "But I'll say this: God has forgiven me for some serious sins."

The HBO special was a mistake for me. Rather than crediting the glory to God and directing the story to our ministry, HBO focused on the tough guy. This was not my intention, nor was it to have them mention names and things written about me long ago and by now mostly forgotten. I gave testimony to being a mob "wannabe" who was saved by the love of God and family. They, in turn, said my paying off my debts amounted to buying my way out of the mob. It was ridiculous. You have to be *in* the mob before you can try to get out.

The HBO special attracted the attention of Geraldo Rivera, who was planning a special called *The New Godfathers*. His producer, Wayne Darwin, phoned and asked if I would play the part of an old-style mob boss preparing to go to prison.

Why not? Neither Patty nor I had slowed the pace of our real work, and once again paying for essentials had become a struggle. We could use the money.

The theme of *The New Godfathers* was the decline of the mob, how the recent jailing of so many top bosses had left a leadership vacuum. In addition, the dwindling respect and loyalty the new, younger bosses could command. Most devastating had been the profusion of rats. Guys facing long stretches in prison no longer adhered to *omerta,* the code of silence. Instead they tried to save their own hides by snitching on higher-ups.

After the filming of *The New Godfathers,* Geraldo took me aside and said, "You're a natural actor. You should get into this business."

I didn't buy the "natural actor" comment. My role in *The New Godfathers* had been easy, playing a character not dissimilar to many I'd often met. Also, I considered acting no more than effectively portraying a lie, and before the near-death experience I'd been down that road countless times.

However, Rivera hadn't been the first person to suggest I might have acting ability. As a chauffeur for Peter DeBlasio, I'd met Danny Aiello and Tony Danza and each, after hearing my voice, said there were parts for me in films.

"I'm serious," Tony Danza said. "Go find yourself an agent."

"Yeah, yeah." I shrugged off the advice.

Now, though, pawing through the Want Ads, I saw an "Actors and Actresses" listing and called the number. An agent named Bruce Kivo answered. He listened to me for maybe fifteen seconds and said, "You've got a great voice. Come right down to the office."

I mentioned to Don Swantek what Kivo had said, and Don smiled. "He's going to sell you a headshot," my friend predicted. A headshot (a photo) can be the first gimmick in an expensive portfolio would-be actors carry around hoping for a big break.

The next morning I drove to Kivo's office in Manhattan and told him straight out, "You try to sell me a headshot, you're gonna get a headshot."

"Hey, chill out," the agent said. "I'm serious. I love your voice. I've got a movie to send you on."

He produced a few sheets of paper—part of a script—and asked me to read some lines for the role of a godfather named Tony T.

I read and Kivo seemed happier than he had any right to be. He made a phone call, wrote down a name and an address, and said I needed to get over there right away.

The receptionist in the fancy office acted as if she'd been waiting for me all her life. She handed me two sheets of paper called "sides," and told me to study them: more words of Tony T.

Ten minutes later, knowing it couldn't be this easy, I sat in Bonnie Timmerman's sparkling office. A major casting director, though I didn't know it, Bonnie was petite with long black hair and big dark eyes. "Frank Minucci," she said. "Glad to meet you."

I noticed several writeups on her desk about my appearance on the HBO special. Less than an hour ago I doubted that she'd ever heard my name.

"I want you to read for me," she said. "My assistant, Allison, will read the lines Sean Penn has."

"Sean Penn?" I was impressed.

"He's costarring with Al Pacino. The film's called *Carlito's Way*."

My role was a mob godfather named Tony T who was imprisoned on Rikers Island and determined to escape. As Tony T, I'd given yuppie/dirtbag lawyer Sean Penn $1 million to make a payoff to spring me from prison, but Penn has kept the money for himself. To redeem himself, he's ordered to help me escape.

The reading went okay—after all, I'd known plenty of people like Tony T—until I got to the curse words. What had I expected? I mumbled through them and Bonnie asked, "There a problem?"

"I try not to use profanity anymore. Especially in the presence of ladies."

"Frank, this is a script. These aren't *your* words. Besides, I've heard worse from my staff."

To demonstrate, she called me several obscene names and I had to grin. Bonnie had the language down pretty good. "Now," she said, "stop the nonsense. I want you and Allison to run through the whole thing."

Which we did, pretty well, I judged, from the smile on Bonnie Timmerman's face. "Call Martin Bregman," she told Allison. "Tell Martin we have our Tony T."

You're hired, I thought, imagining how happy Patty would be. I had a lot to learn about the movie business.

"Frank," Bonnie said, handing me more pages. "Take these home and study them. Come back here next week at this time and we'll read again."

I was confused. I thought she'd said they had their Tony T. It's known as a "callback," as Swantek explained that evening. "It's a good sign," he said, "but don't count the money yet."

I memorized the lines for a week, knew them backward and forward, and Bonnie had a camera set up when I returned. I felt confident facing cameras thanks to experience on those television programs, both the ones with Patty and the talk shows.

This time a male actor read Sean Penn's lines, and I've never been so embarrassed. I'd learned the Tony T part just fine, but not Sean Penn's, and when the actor delivered the cue lines I had no idea how to respond.

Bonnie, fortunately, saw humor in my obvious misery. In fact, she laughed so hard it took a minute before she sent me out to a stairwell to study some more. "In thirty minutes," she said, "you *better* know those cue lines." Then, laughing again, "You can do it, Frank. This part is *you*. It can open a lot of doors for you."

Memorizing posed no problem for me. Maybe, I thought wryly, it was all that experience keeping mental track of who owed what on my loanshark rounds. Whatever, when the camera rolled, I actually scared the young actor feeding the cue lines. He thought he was talking with a real godfather.

The office was quiet for a moment when we finished, then Bonnie said, "Messenger it over to Bregman right away."

I knew nothing about Martin Bregman. He had managed such stars as Barbra Streisand, Faye Dunaway, and Candice Bergen. As an extension of representing Al Pacino, he began producing films, and his long list of credits included *Dog Day Afternoon,* for which Pacino won a Best Actor Academy Award nomination; *The Seduction of Joe Tynan, Venom, Scarface,* and *Whispers in the Dark.*

I met Bregman in his lavish Lexington Avenue office the next day. A sixty-two-year-old New Yorker with silver hair, he wore a silk black-and-white checked jacket, black silk shirt, black trousers, and a braided leather belt with a silver buckle. The man was immaculate.

"Hey, babe," he said, "how ya doin'?"

"I'm okay," I said, placing the script on my lap, expecting him to ask me to read.

"That's not necessary, babe," he said. "I saw the tape Bonnie sent. It's hard to believe you've had so little acting experience. I'd guess it comes natural for you. I've read some articles about your 'career.' You've had some life. Still, to deliver those lines with so little preparation . . ."

"I've been before a number of judges. When you do that, you better have your story right the first time. You can't say, 'Hey, that didn't come out right. Give me another chance, willya, Your Honor?' "

"That kinda training could be helpful, I guess."

Bregman began talking about his Brooklyn childhood, and how a few of his boyhood friends grew up to be wiseguys. He asked if I knew this guy or that, and a few names I did. He reminisced for several minutes, then said—I kept hearing it over and over—"You really are a natural. You're gonna be my new workhorse."

Workhorse?

Bregman called Caulfman Studios in Astoria, Queens, where *Carlito's Way* would be filmed, and said to get Pacino on the phone. He pushed the speaker button and a few minutes later the famous actor said, "Yeah, Marty."

"Al, say hello to Frank Minucci. He'll be coming to the studio tomorrow. Befriend him. Show him around. Get the butterflies out of his stomach."

"Fine, Marty. How ya doin', Frank. I'm looking forward to meeting you."

That night I spoke to a youth group in Newark, and the next morning a limousine picked me up at our Ada Drive duplex and drove me to Caulfman Studios, a large modern facility near the Triboro Bridge. A young man and woman carrying two-way radios introduced themselves as my "aides" and said "anything" I wanted to ask them. I couldn't help thinking how much good just the cost of that limo service could do on the street.

The "aides" led me through long halls to the dressing room area, where on various doors I saw the names PENELOPE ANN MILLER, SEAN PENN, and AL PACINO. Between Penn and Pacino was a door labeled FRANK MINUCCI.

The modern dressing room was filled with bouquets of flowers, a basket of fruit, a full-length sofa, coffee maker, telephone, and lighted mirrors. "Congratulations Frank Minucci AKA Tony T," read a card signed Martin Bregman Productions.

This time I figured I had the role for sure. They wouldn't go to all this trouble, the limo and "aides" and my name on the door, if it weren't definite. Would they?

Yes, they would.

"Mr. DePalma and Mr. Penn," the young woman aide told me, "want to see you in thirty minutes. Make yourself comfortable, have some coffee. I'll be back to take you to them."

This time I'd done my homework. Film writer/director Brian DePalma's long list of credits included *Carrie, Body Double, Scarface, Wise Guys, The Untouchables, Raising Cain,* and *Bonfire of the Vanities.* DePalma, just a few years my senior, had grown up in my neck of the woods—Newark. I doubted that we'd run with the same crowd.

Sean Penn I'd actually seen in a movie or two. I judged him a gifted actor. His credits, for someone just thirty-two, underlined claims that here was a major talent: *The Falcon and the Snowman, Colors, We're No Angels, Judgment in Berlin, Casualties of War,* and *State of Grace.* Penn had not yet received an Academy Award nomination. *Carlito's Way* would rectify that.

When I met with DePalma and Penn, it turned out they wanted me to read, this time with Penn.

"Why don't you practice a little first?" DePalma suggested. "Get comfortable before we roll the camera."

"If it's okay with you," I said, "let's just do it."

"Fine," said Penn. He and DePalma seemed surprised.

Penn read from a script. I had to rely on memory. Almost from the get-go I noticed disbelief on the actor's face and judged he was impressed. He reminded me of the young guy in Bonnie Timmerman's office who believed he'd been talking to a real gangster. Well, he had been, and so was Penn.

Sean Penn shook his fist when we finished. "I like this guy," he enthused. "I like this guy."

DePalma stuck out his hand. "Congratulations, Frank. Welcome aboard."

"This mean I got the part?"

"You do now. It's always been Sean's call. For what it's worth, I think he's made the right one."

Amazing. They really would have removed my nameplate. Bought fresh flowers for my replacement.

I called Bruce Kivo and asked what happened next. "I'll work out the money with Universal," he said.

What he "worked out" was $3,500 a week—a bonanza for us and the ministry—and I stopped the mental nit-picking about expenses. I got paid for ten weeks, most of the time doing nothing. Actual filming took ten days total.

I became particularly close to Sean Penn, who impressed me as a caring and compassionate man. He seemed fascinated by my long career as a biker and mobster, but particularly with my ongoing work on the street. The lights of Penn's life were his two-year-old daughter, Dylan Frances, and his infant boy, Hopper Jack. Their mother was his companion, the actress Robin Wright, who played his love interest in *State of Grace.*

Sean confided to me that *Carlito's Way* might be his last acting role, at least for a while. He wanted to try directing and had acquired several scripts he intended to film. One of them, *Crossing Guard,* with Jack Nicholson, had been completed but not yet released.

He says he'll have a part for me in a future movie, and he certainly helped me on *Carlito's Way.* A constant source of encouragement, he kept urging me not to pay attention to anyone but him on the sets we did together. What impressed me the most, however, was the way he befriended my fourteen-year-old son Angelo, treating him as if they were old friends.

I also saw a lot of the quiet, sharp-dressing Al Pacino, who went out of his way to teach me tricks of the trade. The most valuable involved taping other actors' dialogue, leaving blank spaces on the tape for my dialogue, and then delivering my lines over and over in response to the cues.

I'd have been a fool not to pay close attention to this great actor. He had received Academy Awards for *The Godfather* and *Scent of a Woman.*

At the voiceovers for the river scene, I had just finished doing a loop when I heard clapping and loud whistling coming from the back of the studio. There were Al Pacino and Brian DePalma sitting on a couch applauding *me.* Man, that is an experience you don't have every day.

"Just came to watch a pro at work," Pacino said.

"You're gonna go far in this business," DePalma added.

It was almost too much.

Opening night was a big thrill. A limousine delivered Patty and me to the Ziegfeld Theater premier and then to a celebration at the Plaza Hotel. Frankly, we expected good reviews, and we got them.

I wasn't prepared for the impact the film had on my life. More people recognized me and stopped me on the street—"Hey, Tony

T, how ya doin'?"—from this one film appearance than from everything I'd done my entire life. Calls poured into the house, a number of them from mob guys. They had loved the picture and were convinced they could do a better job than I did. "Hey, Frankie," a few of them asked, "can you get me into pictures?"

The movie role actually helped our street ministry, particularly with gang members. Suddenly it was "more cool" to be seen with me.

Sadly, everything wasn't so positive. I had remained in demand by churches and religious groups as a speaker and counselor, but suddenly it all dried up. It turned out my religious associates took offense at the language Tony T used, and said I had compromised my spiritual values for money. I tried to explain that my pay had gone into expanding our ministry. But the damage was done.

Patty and I were heartsick. We called Southern pastors who previously had pleaded with me to speak at their churches, but they wanted nothing to do with me. We tried to explain that, at my urging, Martin Bregman had removed much of the profanity from the Tony T role, but they wouldn't listen. Nor did they want to hear that more people came to ChristWay because of the movie part than had ever sought me out as Brother Frank, especially kids from street gangs.

It wasn't enough for some pastors to blacklist me. They felt compelled to call and say I'd never be welcome in their churches again, and then rudely hang up.

It worried me, wondering if I might have done wrong. Maybe I rationalized, the old Frank Minucci coming back, but after long sessions on my knees, I didn't believe I had sinned beyond forgiveness. Life, unfortunately, is not all sweetness and light, people saying "I love you, Jesus," over and over. Real-life situations in film are unbelievable if characters like Tony T aren't portrayed realistically. I had expected criticism for some of the language used in the movie, but not to this extent.

A refreshing exception to the religious community hostility came from Pastor Fred Reinglas and his wife Judy of the Son Rise Interfaith Church in Staten Island. Judy and Fred telephoned, and invited Patty and me to join their church, and had us over to their home for dinner.

Pastors Fred and Judy spoke with me many times on the phone. I told him after nine years of preaching, praying, feeding and clothing people, I was feeling hurt, betrayed, and angry. After much prayers, we started attending Son Rise Interfaith. The Reinglases shared loving and scriptural truths. I was able to repent, find healing, and reestablished my vows with God. A little more than a year under Pastors Reinglas's guidance, I was reordained. My family and I still enjoy the love and friendship in this great little church.

The role in *Carlito's Way* led to numerous other acting jobs, including parts in *The Cosby Mysteries, Law and Order,* (twice), and *New York Undercover.* I also did commercials for Time-Life, Monsanto Carpet, Burger King, MCI, Pizza Hut, and the NBA.

As I write this, I have just finished doing the lead role in the coming Broadway production of *Brooklyn Blues,* written by Sidney Goldberg and directed by Avi Haufman, before a live audience of potential backers. I was flattered when, after the performance, I was told one backer had offered a substantial sum if he was guaranteed that I'd appear in the part. Other people—including a theater owner and a producer—gave me high praise. What made me most proud was that I wasn't playing a tough guy, but a genuine teddy bear.

So far, "showbiz" has been good for me. No matter what happens, I won't forget the promises I made to God, who saved my life, cured my cocaine addiction, and gave me my family.

The fact is, I struggle with my demons every day. There is always something tempting me to slide back to the old ways. Old cronies tempt me with big money to come back into shadowy dealings, and pretty women—hoping I can help them get into films—offer to compromise themselves.

Parties offer sex, drugs, and dark friendships that I know could lead me back to a decadent lifestyle. I see how I once had been blinded. I need to remember that I know God and to listen to Him.

Life isn't easy when you accept God: things don't change in the blink of an eye. Willpower is needed, and time, perseverance, and faith. A commitment must be made and stuck with, whatever the cost. When an individual falls, he needs to emulate a child and run to his father (God) for forgiveness and the strength to go on. Trust me, I know, God will help. If failure was final, I wouldn't be here right now. I urge people, Get up, start again, you'll grow stronger each time until you'll be able to stand against whatever comes your way.

For a lot of reasons, I preach wherever the door opens for me, all over the country, no matter what denomination. God loves us all. I like the way His Way has brought love and faithfulness to my house. We practice family values and have grown extremely close.

"You're only average" is a pernicious message conveyed to too many of our young people. They are not average, and they must not so believe. There is only one of each of us in the world, and an average can't be drawn from one. Young ones need to be told they are unique, valuable, precious, priceless—if lost, another could never be found. The message is: You are Somebody! and it needs to be continually repeated for the many among us who, like me, lacked self-esteem. We should remember that life is a gift, and its value can be enhanced by a smile or an encouraging word. Helping another's life enriches your own.

The first man I hugged was an AIDS patient who had heard me on the radio and asked if I would visit him in the hospital. I was terrified, in my ignorance, of this horrible disease, but I went because I knew Christ would have gone. I talked with the man— who had no family, no friends, no one—and prayed with him. As I prepared to leave, he said, "Brother Frank, could I ask a big favor from you?"

"Sure."

"Would you please hug me? I don't want to die without someone loving me."

He was too weak to sit up so I had to put my arms under him. "I love you, my brother," I said, "and you can be sure God loves you too." He wept in my arms.

An hour later, I learned, he passed away. He had seemed so grateful when I came to see him that I wanted to learn a little about him. I found out he had been a semipro boxer and, sadly, an IV drug user.

I've learned to answer requests whenever they come. When I

call on God, He doesn't say, "Hey, not now, I'm tired." Instead He puts His arms around me and comforts me with His love, His unconditional love.

Patty and I have our moments, but realize we want to remain together forever. It takes sacrifice, perhaps giving more than one cares to, but loving compromise makes all the difference. We know that distrust, jealousy, and anger are mainly signs of insecurity. If the love between two people is genuine, little can ever come between them.

I love to make Patty smile. She's my friend. She has given me beautiful things—love, a home, my children. When I think of the pain it would cause, any thoughts of even dabbling with my old life quickly disappear. I've learned that love makes one vulnerable; I know, because until Patty I'd run from love all my life.

My sons and I have established a warm, trusting relationship. Salvatore has graduated from business school, and Angelo plays high school football.

Sal has retained his father's name from his mother's first marriage, but he's really been mine since the age of eighteen months, and I do mean mine. Loving him is easy. He was always a good-natured kid with a deep devotion to his mother. We never kept him from his real father, nor did we teach him anything but respect for his dad.

I love all of my offspring. But Angelo, because of his mother's special love for me, has had a profound influence on me. He grabbed my heart right from the start and remains there even now. He is a bighearted youngster who, I like to believe, has been helped by the love he's received at home.

As for me, put me down as being lucky. All the things I longed for have come to me. The secret: I needed to give love, to receive love, and then I needed to accept love.

Making it short and sweet, I'd like to leave readers with two thoughts: If, with Jesus' help, I could turn my life around, then *anyone* can; and there *is* good in everyone—we just need to look for it. Christ and unconditional love can soften even the hardest heart. I'm living proof.

My Wife

You are the breath in my lungs
the rhythm in my heart
the vision in my eyes
the song in my ears
the only taste my mouth enjoys!
You woman have made me complete
and I love you Patty Joy Naimo Minucci.

Thanks!

FAZUL

Epilogue

I'm not about "organized religion." It segregates, its divides, it enslaves, and it is confined by traditions. I am about God's Word and His love for mankind. I believe if a man sees color when he looks on another, he has a diseased heart. Let those who have ears hear what I say. I neither push nor pull when I speak of God, I simply open my heart and let the love God has put there spill out. This last story is in keeping with the vows I've made with Him.

As Mr. Hoffman and I were nearing the finish of this book, I had a series of four heart attacks, three of which flat lined me in January 1996. I was dead over twelve minutes. Each time that I would die I would experience leaving my body and being brought back again.

I saw so many things I could tell you about, but I would need to write another book. Maybe I will. Right now, though, I want to share one of those experiences with you. It's the greatest, most profound thing I've ever known and trust me I've seen some heavy stuff.

I believe God let this happen to me knowing I'd be brassy enough to tell you about it, regardless of what many will say about me. I am a living witness to life after death and it is the single most inspiring reason I will preach to anyone, anywhere, anytime.

I know GOD is REAL and you can take that to the bank.

★   ★   ★

Right after being put in the ambulance, I grew cold, and then very tired. Bob Jacobs, of the NYFD was my paramedic. Other paramedics told me I was very lucky to have him because he was very highly experienced with cardiac cases. As we drove through the deeping snow of the worst blizzard New York had seen in thirty years, I lay quietly praying and hoping I wasn't going to die. Patty was at my side.

Suddenly, I felt a heaviness rest upon my chest and I experienced a slight rush to my head. I knew death was near. I turned to my wife and the paramedic. "This is it, this is the one," I said. I closed my eyes and died, the first of three times. For what seemed only seconds everything went black. I don't remember anything during that time. Then all of a sudden lights came on and I was out of my body looking down at what was happening. I could see my wife struggling with her seat belt trying to get to me. The paramedic was pounding on my chest and my wife cried out, "Tootsie, don't leave. You hold on, don't leave me!"

It was then that I felt this gentle tugging and passed over into a tunnel. I floated rapidly through this tunnel toward a tremendously bright light. The only light in the tunnel was reflected light from the far end. The walls looked like shards of blue, black, and purple glass that radiated in a rainbow of reflected colors. As I came closer to the end, the rushing sound of the wind became still and I saw a beautifully jeweled crown as I emerged through the light end of the tunnel. Just as my eyes began to adjust to the light, I felt something grab me around my waist. My legs felt heavy. I was being pulled into a dark swirling funnel of hot, stinking air that smelled like a cesspool or a tornado impregnated with rotten eggs and sour milk. Pushed, pulled, and tumbled by dark entities, I was helpless. They laughed at me and cursed me, teasing me as they carried me deeper into the darkness.

Suddenly my spirit screamed for Jesus. Psalms 46:1: says, "God is our refuge and strength, a very present help in times of trouble." I knew I was saved in Christ Jesus, but I felt I was in trouble. "Jesus," I yelled. "Lord, take my hand!" I continued to fall away from the light. Had my confessions not been genuine? Was I being punished for compromising my life as a minister of God by entering into the world of show business? My friends were praying for me, my wife was praying for me, and Pastors Fred and Judy Reinglas had brought me back into the fold and God's presence with love and prayer. I had stepped into the world for money, though it wasn't stolen, it wasn't morally clean and my vows were broken.

Seconds after I shouted for God to take my hand, two huge angelic figures, one in blue robes, one in white, glided right up beside me and stopped me from tumbling in the dark storm around me. Shrieking, hissing, and demanding possession of me, the evil forces became enraged and darted in at me, trying to grab me away from the angels. Each angel took my arm and began to lift me up. The angel in white spoke several words and held out his hand, saying "OMALIC" and several other words. Then there was a burst of blinding white light and a rushing wind. It was cool and filled with the sweetness of fragrant flowers; it was lovely to inhale. Clinging to the angels, I put my head down and closed my eyes as we rose higher and higher into the light. A moment later we floated down into a room whose walls on three sides were alive. They moved slowly, like waves of water, revealing angelic faces in their clouded shapes singing praises to God ever so soft and like nothing I ever heard on earth. The floor was unbroken and looked like mother of pearl with moldings of braided green and white jade all around the room. In its corners were spiral columns of black ebony adorned with ropes of spun gold. The columns climbed to a ceiling of unlimited height that faded into the bright light. The fourth wall was no wall at all; it looked like the sky, blue in color and infinite, no measure of depth or height.

It was explained to me that the angel in blue was my guardian sent to me by Raphael, chief of the guardian angels. This angel was called NeHimm and had been with me all my life on earth. He would remain with me until God released him. The angel in white told me he was the Angel of the Lord, come to meet us and bring us here to an outer room of Christ's throne. Those dark entities were collectors of the souls of unconfessed sinners. They were unaware that I had prayed with my friends and pastors Fred and Judy Reinglas and that I had renewed my vows in repentance before God. The Angel of the Lord was absolutely beautiful; his breastplate and necklace were covered with rubies and many other precious gems. He just seemed to glow with light. My spirit was in awe. As I stood in the center of the room, he said, "He who has sent me to bring you here loves you greatly and will soon be with you. Be not afraid for you are in the hands of the Son of God and no evil shall befall you in His house." The Angel of the Lord put his hand on my shoulder and I felt at peace.

A moment later all the walls, the floors, and the columns were filled with faces. Cherubs and Seraphims and angels with many sets of wings covered in jewels came forward in a light glowing like molten gold. Engulfed in the center of the light with everything around Him singing praises came JESUS! I could feel something marvelous happening to me. I felt the warmth of His Holy light penetrate right through me. I felt as if I was being opened up like a book and the contents of my pages thrown onto the huge blue infinite wall in front of me.

How small I felt, how humble my spirit became as it cried out praises to Him. My soul looked on in awe. I could feel His Holiness, coming even before my eyes could see Him. I was bathed in light, shaken, sifted, and separated. My flesh I left on a gurney in the back of an ambulance and God's Holiness was now separating my soul and my spirit.

Then He was there before me, in pure white robes that shimmered like glistening water filled with the reflection of a billion stars. To gaze upon Him was almost impossible, His Holiness was so bright. He wore a crown of gold encrusted with every precious stone I could name. His entire body emitted a radiant light and in that light His angels moved in and about singing praises to His name.

I know my flesh heart was stopped and back in the natural world, but my spirit man could hardly contain itself. I fell at His feet, my soul leaping with joy as it sank into His Holy presence. Jesus moved up beside me, it was difficult to look at him the light was so blinding. My guardian angel moved forward as if talking with Christ, then he moved to one side.

Jesus pointed to the blue wall and said to me, "Look and see. Let your spirit give witness to all you have seen and done and all you have said and heard. Let your soul be the witness to what is revealed and spoken and to all that you have been even unto that which you would hide. You called me and I answered you. I caressed your flesh and it was healed. I called your spirit and it was delivered from the sting of death's sleep. I gave name to your soul and it was saved. The vows you made, you kept neither in your heart or your spirit. Now let your spirit give its record in truth before your soul and be thankful for the Grace of the Father who has granted you this hour."

The angels bowed their heads. I felt an overwhelming pain, heavier than one feels when a loved one is taken away. As I glanced at Jesus, I saw tears rolling down His cheeks. All of a sudden I could feel the aching pain in His heart for me. I've never known anything like it. I fell to my knees clutching my chest, then on to my face sobbing uncontrollably for forgiveness. He reached down and took my hand in His and lifted me up. When I looked in his eyes a warmth filled my being and the pain left me. I knew without a word that I was forgiven. My being was touched and I felt euphoric, a wonderful sense of being loved. His presence calmed my spirit and soul and He spoke to me.

"Listen to the one who speaks to you in the heart. His voice is Holy and bares the truth of Me. You must be led by Him, follow Him in all that He instructs. Be not swift to take flight; your wings are being strengthened. Keep your vows and walk righteously. In the past you have strayed from the path chosen for you. Your cry was answered even as death touched your flesh, and you were restored. I am the God of Abraham, Isaac, and Jacob. I am the God who gives life to dry bones. I am the God who has breathed life into mankind throughout the scriptures . . . again . . . and again, and again and I have done the same unto you. Obey now my son. I have poured out My love and My grace to cover your transgressions and doubt. Believe! Give the Oracle of God a burning place in you. This you must do and fill your heart with much prayer and thanksgiving. Let my words be a lamp unto your feet. Tell others of this blessing, tell them the God of Abraham, Isaac, and Jacob has given you your life. For I am that I am, I am the God of Mercy. I am the God of Grace. I am the God who gives life . . . say God has touched my life . . . say I was put down but

God has raised me up again . . . again . . . and again. For His power is almighty and everlasting.

"Speak to those who seek me, not from your flesh but from your heart with My Spirit that I give unto you, listen to His voice. Tell them I have sent the fires and they burn even now as I speak and they shall spread across all the Earth giving witness to the power of My Spirit to the saved and the sinner alike. Tell them this is what the Sovereign Lord says:

Those whose hearts cry out to me in Holy reverence;
Those who have not forgotten the poor; Those who have remained as
   the potters clay;
Those who will fall down before me and repent as David did;
Those who love their neighbor as they do themselves;
These will be my remnant, these will I call my Bride.

"In these days, even now My Spirit shall shake all the living world and there will be a great awakening in the souls of men that they know the signs. Let those that have ears hear and those who have eyes see. Go and tell them to make ready for the way of the Lord. You have seen what is to come for all who are yet in the flesh and yet you shall live amongst them, a blessing not many will know. Be kind, beloved, your heart is good. Walk always in peace and faith for what you have seen and heard this day will be your strength in truth. Turn no more from me my son. Loved one of mine by the grace of My Father and the petition of clemency in My blood, you have been restored in My name. I have put the testimony of me in your life . . . go ye now, My loved one, and tell them of me. I have brought my word to life and my word is life for all who believe. You live because I am that I am the Lord your God."

I heard a man's voice, then my wife's, calling my name. I came back through the tunnel, floated over my body. A few moments later there was a sound of rushing air and I was back in my body. I opened my eyes and I was alive. Just as God had said again and again and again.

PROPERTY OF
HIGH POINT PUBLIC LIBRARY
HIGH POINT, NORTH CAROLINA

Thank you Lord for loving me,
Forgiving me,
Keeping me,
And blessing me.

By Your Grace go I.
The Glory is Yours. Amen.

To contact Brother Frank, please write or call:

Brother Frank
c/o Son Rise Interfaith Church
2000 Richmond Ave.
Staten Island, NY 10314
718-494-PRAY